QUALITY ASSURANCE
IN LONG TERM CARE

Thomas H. Ainsworth, Jr., M.D.

ASPEN SYSTEMS CORPORATION
GERMANTOWN, MARYLAND
1977

Copyright © 1977 by Aspen Systems Corporation

Library of Congress Catalog Card Number: 77-70432
ISBN:0-912862-40-8

Printed in the United States of America.

1 2 3 4 5

Table of Contents

Preface

This book is dedicated to the many nursing home administrators in the United States whose primary motivation has been constantly to upgrade the quality of long term care, and to one such administrator, Basil F. (Bud) Boyce, without whose help the book may never have been written.

A previous book, *Quality Assurance Program for Medical Care in the Hospital,* was written when I was the associate director of the American Hospital Association (1970-1973). Throughout twenty years as a practicing surgeon in Bryn Mawr and Philadelphia, I became increasingly concerned with long term care for the elderly. I served as chairman of the Council on Extended Care for the Hospital Association of Pennsylvania during the early days of the Medicare/Medicaid programs. This provided first-hand knowledge of the problems faced by nursing homes as they attempted to meet the conditions for participation in these federal programs and simultaneously struggled with the reimbursement mechanism proscribed by these federal regulations.

During these same years, Mr. Boyce was actively serving as a nursing home administrator in Michigan and subsequently became president of the Michigan Nursing Home Association. In 1973, I first met Bud Boyce who was then a regional director for First Healthcare Corporation. FHC's new president, George Barratt, had determined that excellence in patient care would become their primary goal for the 66 nursing homes they operated throughout the United States. Mr. Boyce was made vice president for patient care. I was retained as a consultant to evaluate the quality of care then provided and to develop a program that would correct any deficiencies and to assure a continuity of high quality care.

We began with an evaluation of the quality of care as measured by an external audit. Both the Phaneuf audit and Qualpac test instruments were used by a team which included Mary Ann Kopernik, R.N., a consultant in nursing care evaluation. The applications of all seven functions of nursing were evaluated:

1. Application and execution of physician's legal orders
2. Observation of symptoms and reactions
3. Supervision of patient
4. Supervision of those participating in care (except physician)
5. Reporting and recording
6. Application and execution of nursing procedures and techniques
7. Promotion of physical and emotional health by direction and teaching

Excellence of performance was seen in only two functions: application and execution of physician's orders and execution of nursing procedures. The audit revealed that nearly all deficiencies in nursing care could be attributed to one cause: nursing care was *task* and *procedure* oriented. It became obvious to the evaluation team that a change in nursing *attitude* was necessary to improve quality; knowledge and skills appeared adequate. Consequently, the quality assurance program was designed to produce a change from a task and procedure orientation to a *goal* and *problem* orientation to nursing care. This book resulted. It is written as a textbook to provide a methodology and the necessary background information required for implementing a quality assurance program for nursing home care. However, the methodology described for nursing care evaluation can be utilized as an outcome-oriented nursing audit for nursing care provided at any level of long term care (rehabilitation hospitals, nursing homes, etc.).

The program has been field tested by First Healthcare Corporation. It was first implemented in 1975 at River Terrace

Healthcare, Lancaster, Massachusetts by Demetria Machado, R.N., director of nursing services. The program is in operation at the Near North Pavilion, the long term care unit of the Illinois Masonic Medical Center in Chicago, where the author serves as medical director.

The author believes the program described is applicable to any long term care facility whose professional management shares the goal of excellence in the quality of patient care they provide.

Thomas H. Ainsworth, Jr., M.D.
Chicago, 1977

Part I

The Need for
Quality Assurance Programs

Chapter 1

The Age of Accountability

The decade of the 1970s has witnessed the dawning of the age of accountability in the United States. Public accountability has become the watchword. Witness Watergate and its effect on politicians. Witness Ralph Nader and his effect on the automobile industry. Witness consumer boycotts and their effect on commerce. Witness the Viet Nam War and its effect on the military. Witness Public Law 92-603, the Social Security Amendments of 1972, and its effect on the health delivery system.

Critics may view this sudden concern for accountability as a desperate clutching at a last straw—an attempt to stay the inevitable disappearance of a laissez faire, free enterprise culture. Optimists will describe the public's demand for accountability as the necessary maturing of a democracy, the existential realization that freedom and responsibility cannot be separated.

The demand that the health care system be included in public accountability is due to the fact that access to our health care system is now viewed as a utilitarian necessity. The public believes that it does make a difference whether or not a person has access to health care services. While good health is not a right, access to care when one is sick is considered a right. Since World War II, the American public has been constantly subjected to glowing accounts of each medical breakthrough as it has occurred. We have raised the expectations of the public, perhaps beyond the ability of our present system to deliver it; but we have also created a public confidence in the system, that once access is attained, the quality of care will be good. Access appears to be the main concern of the public, and cost is seen as a growing barrier to access. The public has demanded, and Congress has responded

3

with, a search for various alternatives to cost control. Both the providers of health care and the public appear to agree that cost control mechanisms must not interfere with quality of care. Public Law 92-603 is an attempt at cost control without interference with quality.

Public Law 92-603 is the most extensive piece of health legislation ever enacted. It was introduced in the Ninety-first Congress as an attempt to correct some of the inequities of the original Medicare/Medicaid law. But during its four-year course through the legislative mill, it was constantly changed and expanded to reflect an increasing congressional awareness of the public's demand for accountability. The final Senate/House compromise version of the bill (H.R. 1—Ninety-second Congress) not only proscribed new conditions for participation by providers in the current Medicare, Medicaid, and Maternal and Child Health Care programs, but also created the blueprints for the control mechanism for any future national health insurance program, whether it takes the form of an expansion of Medicare/Medicaid or an entirely new approach to universal health care coverage. The Conference Committee delegated to the Secretary of Health, Education, and Welfare the task of coordinating the present and future control mechanisms. But they also released a special report to assure that the intent of Congress would be clear to those who would draft the regulations implementing the law.

The final regulations for the current control mechanisms—new conditions for participation in Medicare and Medicaid programs—were released by the secretary of HEW in November 1974, to become effective February 1, 1975.* The delay in releasing the final regulations was to assure that they would be compatible with regulations implementing § 249F of the law, the Professional Standards Review Organizations (PSROs)—the future control mechanism.

---

*Implementation was subsequently delayed by the secretary until July 1, 1975, and further delayed by a temporary injunction obtained by court action brought by the American Medical Association against HEW. This court action was withdrawn when HEW agreed to reissue the regulations with modification of the admission certification requirements.

This PSRO section was introduced as an amendment to the original bill in August 1970 by Senator Wallace Bennett of Utah; throughout its stormy legislative history it was referred to as the "Bennett Amendment." The concept of creating PSROs as the future control mechanism for federally financed medical care programs was based on the success in controlling overutilization of health care benefits by organizations of physicians, known as foundations for medical care, in rural California. These foundations were formed by practicing physicians in that state during the 1950s to compete with a new type of medical care delivery system introduced by the Kaiser Corporation for its employees. The Kaiser plan offered total health care benefits to its enrollees for an annual premium of little more than most health insurance plans were charging for benefits covering only in-hospital care. The Kaiser system (later known as the original model for Health Maintenance Organizations) combined an insurance company, a hospital, and a closed panel of physicians working as a group practice. A single corporation ran the insurance company and the hospital facilities; this corporation contracted with the physician group to provide medical services (corporations were prevented by state law from "practicing medicine" in the 1950s). The contract with the physician group contained a financial incentive not to overutilize benefits. The physician group was paid an annual capitation fee for each enrollee to cover all his medical needs. At the end of the year any unused part of the capitation fee could be kept by the group. If use of benefits exceeded the capitation fee, the group was expected to provide this care free of charge. This financial incentive worked; the Kaiser plan experienced a 50 percent reduction in days of use of acute, short term hospital care. Consequently, their lower premiums caused a serious economic challenge to the usual fee-for-service type of medical care system.

The solo practicing physicians in California met this economic challenge (as well as the challenge of group practice) through their county medical societies. They approached insurance companies with the proposition that if the insurance benefits were expanded to cover office practice as well as in-hospital care, the physicians would form voluntary organizations—foundations for medical care—to control the use of benefits through peer review of all insurance claims by their physician members. This utilization control mechanism also worked; foundations achieved the same 50 percent reduction in use of acute, short term hospital care by the mechanism of retrospective denial of claims which the peer group believed represented overutilization or was not medically necessary.

The success of these foundations in achieving utilization control was the basis for the PSRO concept of the Bennett Amendment. If local practicing physicians could do this in California, why not mandate this type of control throughout the country? Senator Bennett, a Republican, probably believed that the other alternative, the HMO concept, would not be accepted by the majority of the public. And doesn't the PSRO concept, after all, still represent a responsible self-control by a free enterprise system of medical care?

This last question was not seen as rhetorical by organized medicine; they answered with a resounding, No! Most physicians viewed it as being "deputized" against their will as the policeman to watch over the government's health care dollars. But after long and bitter debate, and when finally convinced that Congress was adamant in imposing some type of control to slow the rapid escalation of the cost of these federal health programs, the majority of physicians swallowed the bitter pill because it did permit practicing physicians to conduct the control mechanism. (Only practicing physicians can make the final determinations of medical necessity in PSROs.)

The amendment also has had other critics. Consumer advocates charged that it was like asking the fox to watch the hen house. Others have questioned whether the success in California, where the competition with HMOs was great, can be repeated in other areas of the country where there is no competitive incentive. The consensus has been, however, to wait and see; few believe Congress will be willing to seek alternatives until this mechanism has been tried.

It was essential, therefore, that the regulations implementing the new conditions for participation in the current Medicare and Medicaid programs be designed as intermediate steps in the development of a PSRO system. Section 1155(e) of the PSRO section mandates that PSROs delegate review to physician committees of institutions capable of demonstrating effective utilization review programs. For hospitals, the new conditions for participation in Medicare and Medicaid do provide an orderly transition step, because the new utilization review plans which hospital medical staffs must implement contain the identical programs which will allow them to achieve delegated review when the PSRO becomes active in their community. The new conditions for participation mandate three new programs—two concurrent (that is, occurring while the patient is hospitalized) and one retrospective (that is, implemented following discharge of the patient). The concurrent programs require mechanisms to certify that all admissions to hospitals are medically necessary and that the hospital is the appropriate level or site of care—that is, that care could not reasonably have been provided outside of a hospital without interfering with the quality of care. The second concurrent program is a continued stay review. Utilization review committees of hospitals must review the need for continued stay in a hospital at the fiftieth percentile of regional norms for length of stay for specific diseases or problems. (That is, based on statistical data accumulated in a particular region of the country, an individual patient's continued stay must be reviewed when ordinarily 50 percent of the patients with that same disease could have been discharged.) The attending physician must justify to his peers that continued stay is necessary for his patient because of complications, a change in diagnosis, or an additional problem specific to the individual patient. The retrospective review program requires that the patterns of care be evaluated through the peer review process. Specifically, medical care evaluation studies must be performed which review the hospital's admissions, lengths of stay, appropriateness of ancillary tests and services performed, and medical audits of quality of care.

For the nursing home, unfortunately, the new conditions for participation do not mark an orderly transition to the type of review which will eventually be mandated under PSROs. Utilization review plans for nursing homes do not permit employees of the nursing home to participate in the utilization review program—a limitation not imposed upon hospitals. The Social Security Amendments of 1973 provided a technical amendment which did permit hospital employees to be actively involved in the utilization review program. This did not apply to nursing homes.

Consequently, a "catch 22" exists. Nursing homes are required to have physician utilization review plans in operation, yet are unable to employ physicians to perform this function, even though they are required to employ a medical director who is responsible for controlling the appropriate utilization of resources.

Why have nursing homes been so discriminated against in relation to hospitals? The answer again lies in the area of public accountability. The answer apparently lies in the poor public image of the nursing home industry in general. Recent publications, so-called exposés of the nursing home industry, have publicized many of the intolerable conditions existing in the operation of a small number of nursing homes, and these specific instances of poor care and poor management have, by implication, been generalized to include all nursing homes. Despite the personal protestations of Senator Moss, the Chairman of the Senate Committee on Aging, this poor publicity has been escalated in the public's mind to condemnation of all nursing homes. Such bad public relations is an added challenge to the entire industry, the majority of which are concerned, well-motivated individuals and institutions.

If nursing homes are to assure the public that the care they provide is of high quality and cost effective, mechanisms must be developed that can formally document their performance. This is why there is a great need for a quality assurance program to be implemented in all nursing homes. Not only will the quality of care be documented, but the programs themselves will provide the mechanism of continued improvement, even where the quality of care now meets reasonable standards. The documentation of the quality and cost effectiveness of care through quality assurance programs will also provide the data needed by the nursing home industry to substantiate its demands for adequate reimbursement mechanisms. Well-controlled studies have shown that, in most instances, the quality of care is directly proportional to the reimbursement level.

Therefore, although quality assurance programs instituted in nursing homes by employees of the nursing home will not satisfy the new conditions for participation in Medicare and Medicaid, they will provide mechanisms for the nursing homes themselves to continue to improve quality of care and meet these other needs.

Nursing homes will have separate utilization review programs. But this need not be considered a total duplication of effort; the documentation of care by the personnel within the nursing home will be the basic data used by external organizations performing utilization review for the home and substantiating appropriate utilization based on quality evaluation.

Chapter 2

Accountability for the Aged:
The Unique Role of Nursing Homes

The modern nursing home has become a unique and necessary health care institution, providing several levels of care in the total spectrum of health care services. Currently, there are two levels of health care provided by the modern nursing home. These have been described as skilled nursing care and intermediate care. Some nursing homes limit their services to a single level of care— skilled nursing facilities (SNF) or intermediate care facilities (ICF). Larger nursing homes incorporate both levels of health care service under one roof and management, and others provide a health-related service known as residential care. All three levels of care include patients of all ages, but predominantly the facilities, management, and services are organized for the aged.

Unfortunately, these levels of care have been determined to a large extent by reimbursement mechanisms in federal programs, rather than being specifically based upon patient needs. However, there is a general parallel related to the intensity and amount of nursing care required. A skilled level of care has been defined for reimbursement purposes as the care which requires the services of a registered nurse on a daily basis. Intermediate level of care is defined as that which does not require the services of a registered nurse on a daily basis. If the patient requires the services of a skilled nurse only on alternate days or three days a week, this is defined by reimbursement mechanisms as intermediate care.

Currently incorporated within the skilled level is another level of care which was created by the extended care benefits for Medicare in 1966. This was called extended care or ECF. Unfortunately, many skilled nursing homes, in order to meet the new government standards for the ECF level of care, had to upgrade their facilities and services to, in a sense, become small "hospitals." This law resulted in the establishment of approximately 350,000 extended care beds in the United States certified as meeting the requirements of the Medicare program. But, because of inappropriate administration of the program largely due to actuarial errors in the estimate of cost and subsequent problems in reimbursement, scarcely more than two percent of these 350,000 beds were ever occupied at one time by Medicare beneficiaries. The purpose of creating the ECF level of care was to decrease the length of stay in acute short term hospitals. It was a rational concept, but, unfortunately, the administration of the program made it easier to keep patients requiring this level of care in an acute hospital than to transfer them to a nursing home capable of providing this level of care.

Consequently, in 1974 the ECF level of care was dropped from reimbursement formulas and incorporated into the new definition of the skilled level of care (SNF). The extended care level, however, will undoubtedly continue within the spectrum of health care services. As defined by the private sector, patients best cared for at this level require the same nursing care services as provided in an acute short term hospital, but do not require the ancillary services usually found within a hospital, such as operating rooms, sophisticated lab, and x-ray equipment.

The effect of the new conditions of participation for Medicare and Medicaid and the PSRO program mandated by Public Law 92-603 will probably lead to two levels of care being provided under the same hospital roof—acute short term hospital level of care and extended skilled nursing level of care. Utilization review requirements will produce a decreased length of stay at the acute short term hospital level. It will also result in many patients now hospitalized for diagnostic procedures having these tests performed on an ambulatory basis. Consequently, the total number of beds in the United States now allocated to acute short term hospital care will probably be 25 percent in excess. Hospitals will, therefore, be required to determine some other use for those beds, and it is natural to assume that in the next few years hospitals will begin to see this extended skilled nursing level of care as a hospital-based level. This development should result in nursing homes' experiencing an increase in the length of stay in both

skilled and intermediate levels of care and a greater percentage of
the aged in their patient populations.

To understand the unique role of the nursing home in the care
of the aged, it is helpful to review the historical development of
our institutional health care services which has led to the creation
of the modern nursing home. The following historical review was
written by Basil F. Boyce and is reprinted with his permission.*

As early as 6th century B.C. there were institutions existing that specialized in care for the aged, but it was not
until late in the Middle Ages, the time in European history
between classical antiquity and the Italian Renaissance,
that legislation was adopted by the Church of England for
this purpose. The church's concern and involvement for
the aged was loosely provided for in 1535, but it was the
"Poor Law" of 1601 which was actually the foundation for
public relief and welfare. The law authorized a tax levy to
support the poor and classify the type of attention needed
for various classes of dependents.

The first Almshouse, as they were known, was built in
Bristol shortly after the "Poor Law" was put into effect
and was described as a building housing "convenient
dwellings" for the sick, aged, and feeble. The success of
this institution stimulated development of other Almshouses and further legislation related to them was
enacted. The provision taken by the Almshouses was that
the position and condition of the residents be "less desira-
ble than that of the poorest self-supporting laborer," a
concept that eventually led to an inferior approach to the
care of the aged. This concept finally was publicly damned
in England by the outraged citizenry because it had
become apparent that the aged and feeble were being
haplessly thrown together in the Almshouse with, among
others, alcoholics, drug addicts, orphans, the hopelessly
sick, and the insane.

The American colonies adapted England's laws and
practices relevant to the care of the aged, and the prob-

---

lems that were inherent in the English system were inherited, as well, by the American system. Early in the 19th century, public disgust in the United States for the old Almshouses finally brought about the separation of the various classes of their inmates and the gradual development and establishment of institutions which would eventually specialize in the care and treatment of those other than the aged. The first hospital in the United States, the Pennsylvania Hospital in Philadelphia, was established in 1751. The Almshouses became, at last, homes that were exclusively operated for the care and benefit of the aged.

The early Almshouses in this country were under the complete control of the local governments and, in some instances, existed only because the counties were required by law to provide them. The administration of the Almshouses was generally of low quality, controlled by local political organizations. The objective of the county was to operate on as small a budget as possible, and the Almshouse often used its residents to operate a farm, or do other tasks with the objective of minimizing county costs.

In the long run, Almshouses provided an unsatisfactory solution to care for the aged, with the staff limited in number and usually untrained, and the buildings poorly designed and functionally inoperative. Subsequently, the Almshouses could only provide a minimum amount of care for their senior residents. These facts brought about the need for what is now known as the nursing home, where a resident is provided with a wide range of services, including medical care.

The needs of society at the turn of the century were in a state of transition and flux, and the Almshouses needed to change with the times. They had become very unpopular since they did not satisfactorily meet the needs of the prevailing society. Pressures finally developed in the 30's which culminated in legislation by the federal government reducing the number of Almshouses in the nation.

As the aged left the Almshouses, boarding houses (usually converted residences providing only room and board and not medical care) were organized to care for the senior citizens. It was not until the early 40's, however, that these boarding houses began to offer nursing care. Residents of these private institutions increased substantially throughout the 40's, both relatively and absolutely, so that boarding houses and public institutions for the care of the aged finally gave way to the present day nursing home.

Today nursing homes have evolved to the point where they have become basically institutional solutions to specific health care problems of the aged and by those short-term patients who require minimal or limited nursing care.

Through the years, many major developments in medical knowledge in the field of geriatrics, or care for the aged, have resulted in the fact that the life expectancy for the average individual since 1900 has risen from 47 years of age to more than 72 years of age.

The number of aged in this country continues to grow as people live longer. Costs of medical care provided in institutions have also rapidly increased, due primarily to the explosion of medical knowledge and technology in the last 30 years. With this high cost of hospital care and services, the nursing homes have developed the capability of providing high quality nursing care and services at one-third the cost of the hospital.

With the advent of Medicare and Medicaid coverage, the nursing home industry experienced a period of phenomenal growth. In 1939, there were only 1,200 nursing homes and related facilities. In 1968 two years after the enactment of these federal programs, there were over 19,000 with approximately 880,000 beds. In 1975 there were over 26,000 homes with 1.2 million beds, exceeding the number of beds in short-term hospitals. Although a reflection of the changing age distribution of the population, this fact also reflect the changes in the reimbursement policies of insurance companies and government agencies.

Currently, health care in the United States is provided for by a kaleidoscopic melange of individuals and institutions: private physicians, group practices, clinics, hospital out-patient departments and emergency rooms, hospitals, teaching and research institutions, extended care and rehabilitation facilities, nursing homes. Although there is some informal cooperation, these various elements are not linked together in any systematic way. They operate independently and autonomously, each being responsible for only a small portion of what might be called "total care" of the patient. As a result, no coherent effort has been made to utilize our scarce health resources economically and efficiently. However, Public Law 92-603, the Social Security Amendments of 1972, and Public Law 93-641 are attempts on the part of federal legislators to develop a more coordinated system.

These new laws regulating the health care system should lead to more cooperative efforts between hospitals, nursing homes, and other freestanding health care institutions. Public Law 92-603 brings all institutions under the same regulatory mechanisms. Public Law 93-641 will lead to the development of regionalized health service agencies responsible for developing regional plans for providing comprehensive services to a specific geographic area. The numbers and types of beds and services in various types of facilities will be controlled through implementation of state certificate of need legislation and the control of federal dollars for the construction of facilities and supportive services. The effect of such legislation will increasingly place accountability for care of the aged on the nursing home industry. It is important, therefore, that quality control programs for nursing home care be based on a true understanding of the nature of the aging process and the particular effects of disease upon the elderly. The following chapter, therefore, will review the process of aging, the effects of institutionalization on the aged, and explore the unique nature of nursing care for the elderly.

Chapter 3

Nursing Care for the Elderly

THE PROCESS OF AGING

The process of aging continues to be the subject of keen interest and research. The search for the cause and means of retarding the aging process continues to stimulate the present day "explorer" with the same intensity that spurred our ancestors continually to seek the fountain of youth. Research has, of course, given great insight into the physiological change associated with aging, and these normal biological changes are becoming better understood. Further research into cell metabolism will probably lead to a total understanding of the aging process. We do know that the total number of cells decreases approximately 30 percent between youth and old age. The older cells are somewhat larger, so that the decrease in total body mass is somewhat less than the percentage of total number of cells. There also appears to be a decrease in basal oxygen utilization in direct proportion to the decrease in active cell mass. We, therefore, assume that total metabolic activity of the residual cells remains essentially unchanged. In some systems a reduced functional efficiency can be demonstrated even though the gross functional unit appears to remain intact. For example, there is a delayed nerve conduction time in the elderly. On the other hand, some physiologic systems totally lose their function. There is usually a complete loss of accommodation of the lenses during the fifth decade of life and the cessation of ovulation at the climacteric. It is assumed that if a particular function requires a certain cell mass, with the reduction in the total number of cells, there must be a larger percentage of cells that are constantly in use; there is less time for rest. The fewer cells in the elderly must work longer and under more compulsion. These physiologic changes leave the elderly without the reserves possessed by younger individuals necessary to react to the stress of living.

EFFECTS OF INSTITUTIONALIZATION ON THE AGED

The institutionalization of the elderly has recently been seen as a source of extreme stress. Studies indicate that relocation of the elderly individual from his normal environment results in a high mortality rate within the first year of transfer into an institution. Greater emotional as well as physical stress occurs from lack of preparation for the move. The nature and extent of the transition difficulties as a result of a move from community to a nursing home and the impact on the individual's behavior have been the subject of much study, particularly by psychologists and sociologists. The findings of some studies have indicated that the death rate for older people shortly after admission to nursing homes is high. However, because it is often declining physical health which precipitates the move to the institution in the first place, it is difficult to determine the extent to which institutionalization per se and the attendant stresses in the psychosocial realm contribute to the high death rate.

Aldrich studied the death rates of a group of aged patients who were moved from one facility to another because the first facility was closing. The relocation resulted solely from administrative necessity, and not from changes in the individual's health or family relationships. In every case the patient was moved to a home which was judged to provide equal or better care than the original home. Anticipated death rates, calculated from records at the home, were compared with actual death rates during the first year following transfer. Anticipated mortality (had the residents not been relocated) was 19 percent. Actual mortality was 32 percent. Most of this overall increase for the year was attributable to a higher rate during the first three months following relocation. During this period the actual rate was more than three times as high as the expected rate.[1]

When a person moves from a familiar environment to an unfamiliar environment, he must attend to, receive, and process more stimuli in order to function safely and effectively in that environment. This demands greater activity of cells in the central nervous system. If, in addition, the new environment is perceived as threatening in some way, anxiety will result. Rollo May defines anxiety as "the apprehension cued off by a threat to some value which the individual holds essential to his existence as a personality."[2] This anxiety triggers a sympatho-adrenal medullary response: cardiac output increases, respiration increases, the central nervous system is aroused, and the liver mobilizes glucose. All of this obviously increases the workload of the cells. There are numerous potential threats to essential values when a person enters a home for the aged or a nursing home, any of which may create anxiety and increase physiological demands.

Lieberman compared a group of institutionalized old people, a group on the waiting list for the same institution, and a community group not on a waiting list. From a series of interviews, he obtained data about several areas of psychological functioning.

> Effects that have been frequently ascribed to institutional living (lower future time perspective, increased psychological distance from others, and increased feelings of despair) are here reported as aspects of the waiting period, implying that these psychological qualities may articulate more to the symbolic meanings and fantasies surrounding institutionalization than to the actual experience of institutional life.[3]

Lieberman observed crises about separation, loss, and rejection during the waiting period. He suggests that some of the efforts being invested in the correction of deficiencies in institutional environments might be effectively expended in working with the aged person in the critical months before he is institutionalized.

Goffman has defined a "total institution" as one which "is a place of residence and work where a large number of like-situated individuals, cut off from the wider society for an appreciable period of time, together lead an enclosed, formally administered round of life."[4] Nursing homes have many of the characteristics of total institutions, though most would not rate so high on totality as would most prisons or state psychiatric hospitals. The characteristics of the total institution result in dehumanization of the inmate or patient. Some of these characteristics are:

- Handling of blocks of people by bureaucratic means
- Basic split between a large managed group and a small supervisory group
- Indefinite duration of institutionalization
- All or most segments of living occur in one setting—a single building or group of buildings on the same plot of ground
- The application of industrial production techniques to human affairs, e.g., treating persons as categories (admissions, transfers, deaths)
- Disregard for the person's normal privacies—person constantly with people; no time to be alone
- Decreased responsibility of patient for own domestic arrangements
- Stripping of self-identification, e.g., assignment of a number
- Personal possessions handled by others without patient's permission
- Regimentation; activities governed by a routine and measured pace[5]

Vail states that dehumanizing practices reduce the following human capacities:

- Peace of mind, sense of individuality, and self-worth
- Horizons of wisdom and personal growth
- Adulthood
- Hope for the future[6]

The communal living of the institution itself can also be a hazard to the elderly, particularly in the early days of institutional life when the emotional and physical stresses of the move itself are still applicable. We have mentioned before that during aging there is a progressive decline in adaptive reserve, with the total number of parenchymal cells reduced by 25 to 30 percent. These fewer cells possessed by the aged must work longer and under more compulsion. When additional demands are made, there are fewer well-rested cells ready to meet the demand. For example, there is a decreased ability of bone marrow to increase white cell production in response to infection. This may be of considerable significance when the aged person in a new environment and in proximity to a larger number of people is exposed more frequently to organisms to which he has less acquired resistance; he is less able to cope adequately with infection.

High quality nursing home care should, therefore, have as a primary goal elimination of emotional and physical stress. The environment should be designed to avoid the characteristics of the "total institution" enumerated above. The facility should be designed to permit maximum privacy for the individual, and the organization designed to maximize individualization of activities and "routine" care. For example, the patient should be encouraged to bring with him and surround himself with those possessions with which he is familiar and accustomed.

Whenever possible, the patient should actively participate in planning for the period of nursing home care. Choice of home, discussion of goals and duration of stay, and preliminary visits to the nursing home should be included in the preparation for the move. This active participation by the patient can eliminate much unnecessary stress.

THE UNIQUE NATURE OF NURSING CARE FOR THE ELDERLY

The nurse must be alert to the hazards of institutionalization, for they may truly be a matter of life or death to the aged patient. The nurse who understands physiologic changes of aging and the extreme effect of stress on the elderly will have greater insight into the ways nursing care can anticipate and prevent stressful situations and, therefore, provide a much higher quality of nursing care. There are two basic tenets that describe the uniqueness of nursing home care as opposed to care rendered by nurses in hospitals:

1. Nursing home care places a greater emphasis on nursing care than on physician care.
2. Nursing home care, like other long term care, emphasizes restorative care and/or maintenance and support of the patient.

The quality of nursing care is of major importance since it is the predominant health discipline responsible for patient care within the nursing home setting. Nurses exercise greater independence in making patient care judgments. Nurses also are given greater primary responsibility for the supervision and coordination of the total patient care administered.

The patient in a nursing home is usually one whose illness has reached medical stability and is beyond the need for acute care provided in the hospital. He now requires assistance to live with the long term aspects of his illness, so the emphasis in the nursing home is on restorative nursing care, which can be characterized as "wellness oriented." One must identify the positive aspects of health which the patient has maintained and strive to restore the total health potential which remains. In this context, Henderson's definition of nursing care acquires meaningful dimension and should have a greater impact on the nursing practice within the nursing home. This definition states that the unique function of the nurse is to assist the individual, sick or well, in the performance of those activities contributing to health or its recovery (or to peaceful death) that he would perform unaided if he had the necessary strength, will, or knowledge, and do this in such a way as to help him gain independence as rapidly as possible.[7]

Thus, nursing is a health-oriented discipline which shares goals and functions with other health professionals and at the same time possesses unique goals and functions in administering patient care. Nurses fulfill their unique function through a goal-directed, patient-centered, deliberative process.[8] The nursing process has four components, usually performed in sequence. They are: (1) assessment, (2) planning, (3) implementation, (4) evaluation. In practice situations these four components seldom completely separate into discrete entities which neatly follow each other without overlap. This is particularly true in the acute short term time phase of care provided in hospitals. It is less true in the longer time phase associated with care in a nursing home.

Patient care evaluation as part of the day-to-day care of the patient implies reassessment and replanning and new implementation. The patient's progress or lack of progress in meeting his specific goals and objectives in a timely manner are evaluated.

Problems which interfere with achieving each objective are identified, and appropriate change in the nursing care approach is
then made to meet better the goals and objectives. This results in
a dynamic nursing care plan which is always current in its implementation. Nevertheless, there is a definite directional flow which
is crucial to practice, because sound, effective functioning in any
single phase requires the solid foundation of the preceding phases.
The nursing process can, thus, be diagrammed as a continuous
circle.

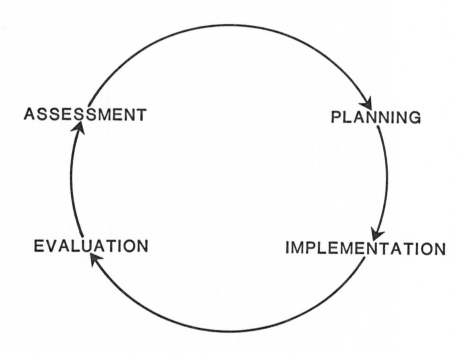

The quality assurance program described in this book combines
this cyclic nursing process with the similar cyclic process used in
the newer methodologies for assessment of the quality of patient
care. The similarities of this concept of the nursing process and
the methodology described for quality assurance programs in
chapter 4 become the basis for the quality assurance program for
nursing home care later described in chapter 5.

Notes

1. C. Knight Aldrich and Ethel Mendkoff, "Relocation of the Aged and Disabled: A Mortality Study," in *Middle Age and Aging,* Bernice L. Naugarten, ed. (Chicago: The University of Chicago Press, 1968), pp. 401-408.

2. Rollo May, *The Meaning of Anxiety* (New York: The Ronald Press Company, 1950), p. 191.

3. Morton A. Lieberman et al., "Psychological Effects of Institutionalization," *Journal of Gerontology,* 23 (July 1968): 350.

4. Irving Goffman cited in David J. Vail, *Dehumanization and the Institutional Career,* (Springfield, Illinois: Charles C. Thomas Co., 1966), p. 58.

5. Vail, pp. 58-77.

6. Vail, p. 32.

7. Virginia Henderson, *The Nature of Nursing* (New York: The Macmillan Company, 1966), p. 15.

8. Ernestine Wiedenbach, *Clinical Nursing: A Helping Art* (New York: Springer Publishing Company, Inc., 1964), p. 23.

Chapter 4

Quality Assurance: An Overview

Parallel to the growing demand for public accountability in the health care field, new methodologies for assessment of the quality of care have developed. These processes have generally been called medical care evaluation studies or, synonymously, medical audit, nursing audit, pharmacy audit, etc. Their development has been by the various disciplines involved, the methodology usually restricted to their single discipline. This has led to fragmentation of the evaluation mechanism by the separate disciplines. But, more recently there has been added emphasis on the necessity for patient care evaluation of an interdisciplinary type. This has paralleled the change in the approach to health care characterized by a growing concern for the total patient as a unique individual and a realization that total care requires an interdisciplinary approach.

To evaluate the quality of care, methods had to be developed to measure quality. Until the recent past, measurement instruments were based on measurements of the *structure* in which care was delivered. Such measurements were applied not only to the personnel providing care, but also to the facilities and services necessary to deliver patient care. Sophisticated and elaborate structure measurements for personnel have been devised over the years. These have included educational requirements for health personnel, licensure, and, more recently, board certification for physicians. Facilities have also been licensed, usually by government authorities, and facilities and services have been accredited by voluntary professional organizations such as the Joint Commission on Accreditation of Hospitals. More recently, government has certified institutions for participation in federal health programs, delegating to state agencies the responsibility for determining whether or not the standards for participation in the programs were met.

THE AUDIT PROCESS

A few years ago, Donabedian[1] at the University of Michigan asked the pointed question, "Do structure measurements alone assure good performance?" The obvious answer is, "No." Since that time the field has developed methodologies for measuring performance as well as the structure, and these new measurement tools have been known as process and outcome measurements. Nearly all quality assurance mechanisms today, therefore, concentrate on these measurements of *process* and *outcome,* that is, quality of performance, in addition to the historical structure measurements.

The methodology used in these performance assessments has generally been based upon adaptations of a medical audit process popularized by Doctor Clement Brown,[2] which is commonly known as the bi-cycle concept, which relates medical audit to continuing education in two continuous cycles. In developing the *Quality Assurance Program for Medical Care in the Hospital,*[3] this methodology was simplified into the following five steps:

A. Criteria development
B. Description of performance
C. Evaluation (Does B = A?)
D. Corrective action (If B does not = A)
E. Reassessment (After D, now does B = A?)

Criteria Development

Criteria are elements of care used as instruments to measure performance—specifically, those elements thought to be essential for high quality care. For measurement purposes, a quantitative *standard* of performance must be assigned to each element. Therefore, a *criterion* equals an *element* of care plus a *standard* of performance. The peer group of health professionals selects the elements and then assigns standards by utilizing their knowledge and experience, recognized experts in a particular field, and the medical literature. A standard may simply state that an element should be performed. For example, such a criterion might state, "An electrocardiogram should be taken before surgery in all persons forty years of age or older (the element) in 100 percent of cases (the standard)."

Standards may also be based upon norms. *Norms* are numerical values obtained by measuring current practice using specific criteria; they describe the range of usual practice in a particular community. Norms vary from region to region within the United States, being affected by such conditions as geography, patient mix, available resources, and practice patterns of physicians in the area. Standards based upon norms are usually stated as the allowable deviation from the median of the norm. For example, length of stay norms from a geographic region in the United States for specific diseases have been compiled by various data discharge abstract services. These frequently are recorded according to age and sex groups and expressed as percentiles of all patients hospitalized for a particular disease. The fiftieth percentile represents the median of the norm; that is, one-half of the patients are still within the hospital. A standard could then be expressed for audit purposes as varying from the twenty-fifth to the seventy-fifth percentile—that is, the allowable deviation on either side of the median of that norm.

Criteria development as a first step in the audit process assures that the audit will be totally objective—that is, the criterion, norm, or standard has been determined before care is measured. Each audit tends to validate the criteria used in the measurement. Thus, criteria should never be thought of as permanent or absolute values; they may be changed, altered, or eliminated as the audit group develops experience in measuring and evaluating care. Standards should gradually be changed to serve as an incentive to increase the quality of care on a continual basis. Experience has also shown that criteria have the most meaning if there is active participation by all practicing professionals involved in the audit process and whose care is being evaluated. This active participation by all personnel in the peer group in criteria development has been shown to produce the greatest change and improvement in behavior of professionals through the use of the audit process. In this sense, therefore, criteria are the yardsticks used by a peer group to set its own goals and objectives for the care they are providing.

Two types of criteria are now being utilized: *process* and *outcome*. Initially criteria for performance were basically *process* criteria; they measured what was done for the patient in the course of treatment. Experience showed that it was very difficult to obtain universal agreement on process criteria by a group of peers. The varied experience of peers was reflected in the inability to determine one best way to treat a particular condition. There has been generally expressed fear that if process criteria were to become too rigid and limited this could lead to a "cookbook" approach to medical care; it would stifle initiative and prevent the necessary innovation which in the past has led to continual improvement in the quality of care.

Because of these concerns, *outcome* measurements have become more accepted as a measurement of performance. It has become much easier to achieve peer agreement on outcome standards than on process standards. Outcome measurements accommodate variation in alternate approaches to treatment according to the training, experience, and prejudices of individual practitioners; they permit this freedom of practice as long as similar or better outcomes are achieved.

The development of outcome measurements has also permitted a mechanism for decreasing the number of cases that need to be specifically analyzed in the peer review process. For audit purposes, if outcomes are good, then there is little need to look at the process by which these outcomes were achieved. This, therefore, serves as a screening mechanism to reduce the number of cases which need to be referred to peer review. Screening mechanisms are seen to be more applicable to health care evaluation than random sampling techniques because of the number of variables in the way a specific disease or problem affects a specific individual. If the product of the health care system were ball bearings which had to meet standards of .0015 of an inch, it would be very easy to use random sampling techniques. Every 50th ball bearing could be measured according to the standards, and if the standards were met, the entire assembly line could be considered to be producing high quality output. In health care, however, there are no two "ball bearings" alike. If the random sampling techniques are used, the peer review group spends much of its valuable time in reviewing perfectly normal care, and the other half of the time they are missing the chance to evaluate poor care that may have been missed in the random sampling selection process. Screening, therefore, permits 100 percent of all cases to be reviewed by the peer group. Process measurements need only be done if outcomes do not meet the standards, that is, do not "pass" the outcome screen.

Description of Performance

Using the medical record or other documentation of performance, the care provided is measured by the criteria developed in the first step. While this can be done by individual chart review by professionals involved in the audit, there has been increasing reliance upon other allied health professionals specifically trained in medical records to perform this measurement. This is accomplished by abstracting each medical record at the time of discharge to show conformance or nonconformance to each criterion as documented in the medical record. For audit purposes, if care is not documented, it has to be assumed that the care was not provided. Consequently, an audit team in its early activity in audit usually produces an improvement in documentation and in the quality of medical records.

Evaluation

Evaluation must be a peer review mechanism. While medical records personnel or even computers can determine when care does not conform to criteria, they cannot evaluate whether such deviations represent a deficiency, i.e., suboptimal care. This is because health care is not an exact science. Each individual patient is different, and the disease process varies in each patient. Consequently, treatment also has many variables. For this reason most experts now agree that quality of health care cannot be evaluated on a case-by-case review. It is only as groups of similar cases are evaluated that a pattern of care develops, and the pattern is the only reliable measurement of quality. Therefore, medical records personnel usually provide a data display of a group of patients with a similar disease (usually 50 or more) so that the pattern of care can be evaluated. The peer group then evaluates the variations from the criteria and determines whether or not the variations actually represent a deficit. An evaluation of the numbers and types of deficits determines whether a problem area exists. If problem areas are identified, the group then determines the cause of the problem. Further, they attempt to identify whether the cause of the problem is due to deficiencies in performance of personnel or organizational barriers to high quality of care. If performance of personnel is determined to be the cause, they will attempt further to determine whether this is due to a deficit in knowledge, skills, or attitude. The group will then make appropriate recommendations to correct all deficiencies by correcting the cause.

Corrective Action

If the group determines that problems exist and performance is suboptimal, it will determine appropriate corrective action to improve quality of care. The term "corrective action" is not used in the punitive sense. Nor should the quality assurance program itself be considered a punitive program. Most professional health care personnel will respond better to a positive incentive than to a negative incentive. Many times, feedback alone will produce the desired change in behavior. Sometimes, the corrective action used to bring about change in behavior must be an educational program designed to improve the individual professional's knowledge, skills, or attitude. If the deficiency appears to be attributable to a single individual, several individuals, or an entire service, the continuing education program design is usually provided for those who have been shown to need the educational program as evidenced by their continued pattern of suboptimal performance in the area being evaluated. Organizational problems which have been identified in the evaluation process as a barrier to high quality care are referred to the appropriate individuals or groups with suggestions for change in these areas.

Reassessment

After the appropriate corrective action has been taken, its affect on correcting any deficiencies should be assessed by repeating the above steps. If care has not been improved according to the new measurement, then different corrective action should be tried. The process, therefore, becomes cyclic, each audit becoming a feedback mechanism to identify problems in the process itself. For example, if the criteria that were developed for measuring quality of care appear to be inappropriate, they should be changed or altered. If standards were set too high or too low, similar accommodations should be made. When this process is utilized by a peer group involved in the delivery of care at the local level, the mechanism becomes a systematic approach to constantly improving the quality of care. The peer group is actively involved in the management of patient care through the process known as "management by objectives." This management process, like the nursing process described in chapter 3, is best visualized as a cyclic process as described in step E, Reassessment. The other steps A through D can be diagrammed as:

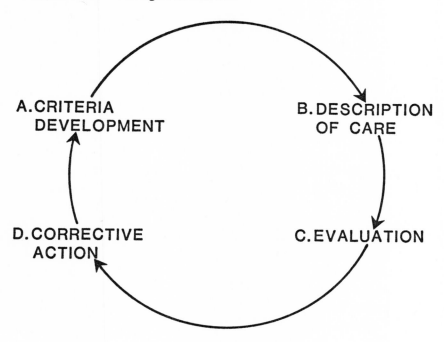

AUDITS AND UTILIZATION REVIEW

Quality assurance programs can also be classified with respect to the particular aspect of care being evaluated. *Audits* (medical, nursing, etc.) are usually confined to the professional aspects of care. They evaluate the application of the knowledge and skills of a single discipline, or the combined disciplines represented in the health care team, to the treatment of a patient's problem. *Utilization review* judges medical necessity, the appropriateness of the level of care being provided, and the efficiency with which care is provided by the health care team. Utilization review is primarily concerned with the cost of care, while audit has more emphasis on the quality of care. However, there is a growing realization that these two processes cannot be separated; in reality, cost of care, access to care, and efficiency with which care is provided are all elements of quality.

CONCURRENT AND RETROSPECTIVE PROGRAMS

Another classification of quality assurance programs is based upon the time-frame in which the care being provided is evaluated. If the evaluation is being carried out while the patient is receiving care, this is known as a concurrent program. Retrospective programs review the care provided at various times after care for an episode of illness has been terminated.

Concurrent Programs

In hospitals, concurrent programs have frequently been confined to utilization review. Since utilization review must be performed on a case-by-case basis and since control of the cost of care is more easily accomplished while the patient is receiving care, utilization review is usually performed as a concurrent program. This is particularly true when the purpose of the program is control of costs. Consequently, most programs required by third party purchasers of care are concurrent. There has been some experimentation with concurrent audit (quality evaluation) of care rendered in the hospital setting, but this has not been generally accepted because of many difficulties encountered with a concurrent audit program. Concurrent audits must, by their nature, use process criteria alone. (Outcomes have not yet been achieved.) The primary objection, however, comes from physicians. As highly trained professionals, they object even to their peers' looking over their shoulder while they are in the process of providing care, and they object strongly to being told what tasks should be performed and how they should be performed. Most professionals, however, are not disturbed by being held accountable for the outcomes of their care and, therefore, readily accept retrospective medical audit.

In long term care, however, concurrent care has an entirely different time reference. In contrast to the eight-day national average length of stay in a hospital, the average length of stay in a nursing home is about 300 days. Therefore, audit of the quality of care in a nursing home is usually, of necessity, a concurrent program. Utilization review is concurrent as well. In the audit of quality of care in a nursing home this longer timeframe also permits outcome evaluation, which is prohibitive in the short duration of care in the acute general hospital. For this reason, it has become necessary to identify several types of outcome criteria, especially when they are used in the audit of long term care.

The term *eventual outcome* (or *ultimate outcome*) is easily understood. This is usually thought of as the eventual outcome of all care rendered either in the hospital or in a long term care facility. Such care is usually evaluated months or years after the end of an episode of illness. It is usually associated with evaluation of the health status of a community or group of patients. The methodology for such outcome evaluation is still in its infancy, and the current state of the art in health care evaluation nationally has prevented any widespread implementation of this methodology except in end-result studies of cancer care.

The term *immediate outcomes* has been used to describe the measurement of the status of the patient at the time of discharge from a specific level of care, that is, at the end of a period of hospitalization or at the end of a stay in a nursing home. Medical care evaluation using immediate outcome criteria asks the question, "Did we accomplish what we intended to for this patient or this group of patients in this level of care?"

The term *intermediate outcomes* applies to specific objectives reached in the course of treatment *within* a particular level of care—necessary intermediate steps in achieving immediate outcomes. The use of intermediate and immediate outcomes is, therefore, most applicable to concurrent audit of care in long term care facilities. In long term care, intermediate outcome measurements can, therefore, be accomplished in a concurrent review program because of the long term nature of nursing home care.

Retrospective Programs

Retrospective review is usually utilized for audit of quality of care because it permits the use of both outcome and process criteria measurements and permits evaluation of a pattern of care. Utilization review programs, however, can also be evaluated retrospectively, and indeed the new conditions for participation in Medicare and Medicaid programs do require that retrospective review study patterns of admission, length of stay, and the appropriateness of ancillary tests and services used in the course of treatment. This requirement is applicable to both hospitals and nursing homes. The PSRO law also requires that institutional profiles be developed by retrospective analysis of patterns of care. The mechanism used by PSROs to monitor institutions to which they have delegated review function will probably ultimately be based on periodic evaluation of institutional, physician, and patient profiles as developed by identifying these patterns of care through retrospective audit methodology. Retrospective audit of the quality of care rendered in nursing homes will probably be limited to studying groups of patients who are treated in a nursing home for similar conditions, such as fractured hips, stroke, senility, etc. These retrospective nursing home audits will look at patterns of care for a group of patients, while concurrent audit programs will be applied to individual patients.

As mentioned in chapter 1, the quality assurance program described in this book will not meet the current federal mandates for utilization review for Medicare and Medicaid programs. Concurrent utilization review programs necessary to meet these federal regulations will be provided by organizations external to the nursing home. However, the concurrent audits described in this text will be designed primarily to evaluate the quality of care provided individual patients during the course of their stay in the nursing home. But, since intermediate outcomes also include a time estimate for accomplishment, the documentation of these continuing concurrent audits will be most helpful for use in the utilization review programs.

The concurrent quality assurance program described in detail in chapter 5 will, therefore, be a concurrent audit of the care received by an individual patient using intermediate and immediate outcome criteria. The methodology will also be problem oriented, and criteria will be developed for each of the patient's identified problems which together contribute to the need for nursing home care. Since the day-to-day care of patients in the nursing home is mainly provided by nursing personnel, the concurrent programs will be a nursing audit, although it will incorporate other allied health professionals involved in the day-to-day care. The program will describe the methodologies for an initial nursing evaluation of the patient to identify his problem, the mechanisms for setting therapeutic goals for the patient (immediate outcomes), mechanisms for identifying and setting intermediate objectives (intermediate outcomes), and mechanisms for prescribing appropriate nursing actions to accomplish these goals and objectives.

The retrospective quality assurance program described in chapter 6 will be a retrospective review of specific diseases treated within the institution. It will be a multidisciplined approach, incorporating physicians, nurses, and other health professionals providing care. It will examine patterns of care rather than evaluate the care provided to an individual patient.

Notes

1. A. Donabedian, "Evaluating the Quality of Medical Care," *Milbank Memorial Fund Quarterly* 44 (July 1966): 166.
2. C.R. Brown and D.S. Fleisher, "The Bi-cycle Concept Relating Continuing Education Directly to Patient Care," *New England Journal of Medicine* 284 (May 20, 1971): 88.
3. T.H. Ainsworth, ed., *Quality Assurance Program for Medical Care in the Hospital* (Chicago: American Hospital Association, 1972).

Chapter 5

The Quality Assurance Program
Part A: The Concurrent Program

The Quality Assurance Program for Nursing Home Care has two aspects, as referred to in chapter 4. The first part (Part A) emphasizes the care of the individual patient; the other (Part B) emphasizes the pattern of care rendered by the institution to all patients. The Part A program is a concurrent program which is carried out while the patient is receiving care. It provides concurrent patient care evaluation (nursing audit) by the use of goal- and problem-oriented nursing care and incorporates concurrent utilization review. The Part B program is carried out retrospectively (although it may include some patients still institutionalized) by periodic evaluation of the results obtained (outcomes) by analysis of the patterns of care provided all patients with the same problems or disease entities. This chapter will describe the Part A program, concurrent review. We will separately address two aspects of concurrent review, nursing audit and utilization review.

NURSING AUDIT

This concurrent review program is based on a philosophy of goal-oriented nursing care. Evaluating how well goals are being achieved then becomes part of the day-to-day care of the patient. This is also problem-oriented nursing care. Each patient is considered as a whole individual who may have many separate problems, the combination of which contributes to the need for nursing home care. Establishing goals and prescribing nursing actions for the alleviation of these problems becomes the nursing care plan for restoring the patient to an optimal state of health.

The nursing care plan is based on the physician's medical care plan for the patient, including an estimate of the patient's restorative potential. Based on this communication about the patient from the physician, the nurse must make an initial assessment of the patient to determine how the professional nursing discipline can contribute to the care of the patient. The initial (and continuing) assessment results in written nursing orders or actions to be carried out by nursing personnel. The nursing care plan is *not* the transcription and carrying out of physicians' orders by nurses!

The initial assessment identifies the patient's individual problems; then goals and objectives can be developed for each problem, and specific nursing approaches to meet those goals and objectives can be formulated. When a nursing care plan is established for each patient, periodic evaluation of the patient's progress can be conducted by the entire nursing care team. Progress, or lack of progress, in meeting the specific goals and objectives, in accordance with the plan, can be identified. When the measured results are not meeting the goals and objectives of the nursing care plan, appropriate changes can be instituted. This ongoing concurrent review produces a dynamic (constantly changing) nursing care plan which is always current because it is based upon the continuing evaluation of the patient's progress.

The nursing audit methodology was created by adapting the cyclic audit process described in chapter 4 to the cyclic nursing process described in chapter 3. This nursing process was made the core of the program, because the primary purpose was to improve the quality of nursing care by emphasizing a goal- and problem-oriented approach. The steps employed in carrying out the elements of this process (assessment, planning, implementation, and evaluation) in the day-to-day care of patients were utilized to produce an ongoing patient care evaluation mechanism. By appropriate documentation of these steps, the process can be evaluated for audit purposes.

The steps employed in each element of this nursing process are as follows:

Assessment

1. Obtain the physician's care plan.

2. Obtain a nursing history and perform a nursing physical examination.

3. Identify the patient's problems.

Planning

4. Set the therapeutic goals for each problem. A discharge plan is written considering these therapeutic goals.

Implementation

5. Nursing actions are prescribed and written to help the patient attain the therapeutic goals for each problem.

Evaluation

6. Nursing progress notes are written periodically to document the nurse's evaluation of the patient's progress in attaining each therapeutic goal.

7. Nursing care conferences are held to permit the entire team to participate in the evaluation, to identify the need for corrective action, to participate in the educational programs designed as corrective actions, to reassess the patient's problems, and to set new therapeutic goals and nursing actions.

Steps 4 and 5 correspond to the criteria development step (A) in audit. Step 6 corresponds to the description of care step (B) in audit. Steps 6 and 7 correspond to the evaluation step (C) in audit. Step 7 provides for the corrective action step (D) in audit. Steps 1, 2, and 3 correspond to the assessment and reassessment step (E) in audit. This correlation of the nursing process to the audit (and utilization review) process in the concurrent program is diagrammed as follows.

FIGURE 5:1

Correlation of the Nursing Process to the Audit Process and Utilization Review in the
Concurrent Quality Assurance Program

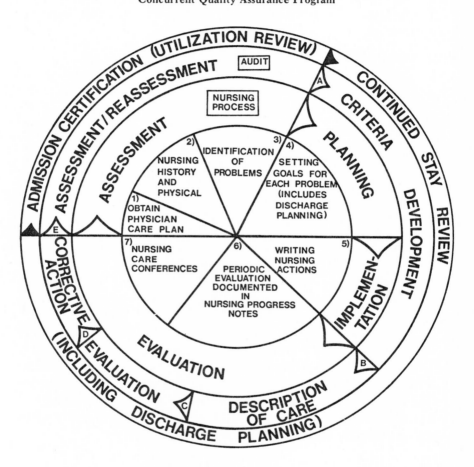

This nursing/audit process is, therefore, carried out in a step-by-step approach to the care of each patient in the following manner:

Assessment

Step 1—The nursing facility will insist that a physician-prepared patient care plan for each patient be documented at the time of admission. Patients should not be accepted in transfer unless this documentation precedes or accompanies them to the facility.

Step 2—The director of nursing service is responsible for the completion of a comprehensive patient care assessment before, at the time of admission, or as soon as possible within the first 48 hours of admission. Such assessment should follow the medical care plan for the patient and result in a specific nursing care plan for each individual patient. This assessment involves the performing of a nurse history and physical examination.

Step 3—The assessment should result in the identification of all the patient's problems. Each of the patient's problems should be identified and numbered. The director of nursing service may delegate these tasks, but must retain the responsibility and function of assigning the initial length of stay for utilization review purposes based on her identification and analysis of the patient's problems.

Planning

The nursing care plan is to be written and is to be problem-oriented. The following format should be followed:

Step 4—Goals should be developed for resolving each problem, based on the patient's restorative potential. A time estimate is to be made for achieving each goal, considering length of stay guidelines.

Implementation

Step 5—Specific nursing approaches (actions) for each problem are to be identified. This will include specific tasks and procedures to be performed by various members of the facility health care team in assisting patients to achieve their goals.

Evaluation

Step 6—A periodic evaluation of the patient's progress will be documented. The method of documentation will be the patient's progress notes and will be used by all professional members of the facility health care team. Maintenance of the patient's progress notes will be the responsibility of the charge nurse in each unit. Frequency of such documentation will depend upon the intensity of illness or care. All documentation should refer to the numbered problems listed on the nursing plan. (A problem list should appear as a separate sheet preceding all progress notes in the patient's medical record.) Each progress note for each problem will contain the following elements of information:

1. **S** Subjective problems and/or complaints by the patient.
2. **O** Observed problems and/or reactions to the treatment process, as evaluated by the nurse.
3. **A** Assessment of the patient's new status in relation to the original goal.
4. **P** Plan for continued treatment. A specific notation should be made of a change or continuation of the nursing order plan for this particular problem.

It is intended that the first letter of each of these progress charting guidelines spells out the acronym SOAP. This acronym will remind the person responsible for the documentation of the necessity of addressing each of these items in each progress note.

Step 7—Patient care conferences. In addition to the periodic evaluation of the patient's progress by the charge nurse (see step 6), the patient's total care will be periodically evaluated by the entire patient care team: director of nursing service, charge nurse, and nurses' aides. These conferences should also be attended by other specialists and those other allied health professionals directly involved in the care of the patient, such as the social worker, physical therapist, etc. In this way, each patient's care will be evaluated in an inservice type educational format at frequent intervals, but at least once every 30 days for the first three months and thereafter at least every 90 days.

Patient care conferences are basically nursing care conferences, but the facility's medical director and the patient's attending physician should be encouraged to attend. Such patient care conferences should also result in a statement of the nursing staff's estimate of the patient's continued need for a specific level of care, skilled, intermediate, or residential. A discharge plan must be written as early as possible within the first seven days of admission. Such estimation will be of great value to the utilization review committee in carrying out its functions.

UTILIZATION REVIEW

This concurrent review program is based on the concept that efficient and appropriate use of health care resources is an element of quality of care. It is, therefore, an important aspect of a quality assurance program. It provides data for use by the facility in its day-to-day management and long term planning, as well as meeting the needs of third party purchasers of care and, more specifically, the federal government Medicare and Medicaid programs.

The utilization review plan will usually be proscribed by federal and state regulations for Medicare and Medicaid and will vary with the type of long term care facility. A utilization review plan for nursing home care developed for First Healthcare Corporation is found in appendix A. This can serve as a model for any nursing home, but will vary in detail with the particular review methodologies proscribed in various PSRO areas.

Fundamentally, the documentation of care that results from carrying out the nursing/audit process provides all data necessary for review of appropriate utilization. These data can be made available to utilization review committees of the facility or those external to the facility. The *assessment* steps in the nursing process documents the appropriateness of the level of care and the medical necessity of admission; this satisfies the requirement for initial certification for Medicare patients. The *planning* step documents the length of stay required to achieve the goals set for each of the patient's problems. Regional length-of-stay norms are usually available as guides in setting the timeframe for achieving each goal. Such planning also permits the writing of a realistic initial discharge plan.

In the *implementation* step, the writing of specific nursing actions, documents the need for a specific level of care. For example, those nursing actions requiring the knowledge and skills of an RN on a daily basis document the need for a skilled nursing level of care. In the *evaluation* step, the nursing progress notes and minutes of the patient care conferences document the necessity for continued stay. Such documentation is an aid to the physician in the initial and subsequent recertification required for Medicare patients. The medical record which results from this goal and problem-oriented approach to nursing care will provide all data necessary for retrospective medical care evaluation studies of utilization patterns.

Chapter 6

The Quality Assurance Program
Part B: The Retrospective Review Program

The retrospective review program is complementary to the concurrent review program described in chapter 5. The primary emphasis of the concurrent review program is nursing care evaluation. The retrospective review program will emphasize total patient care evaluation. The review team will include physicians as well as nursing and administration. Conduct of this program will be the primary responsibility of the medical director of the nursing home or the utilization review committees of other long term care facilities. The program is designed to review the quality of care of all patients admitted to the institution. It is also designed to satisfy the opportunity available under section 1155(e) of the PSRO amendments to Public Law 92-603, to permit the institution to qualify for a delegated review function by the local PSRO for its Medicare and Medicaid patients. For nursing homes, this will probably require the addition of physicians appointed by the local PSRO for participation in the program.

The methodology described in chapter 4 will be utilized. This methodology incorporates the following five steps:

A. Criteria development
B. Description of performance
C. Evaluation (Does B = A?)
D. Corrective action (If B does not = A.)
E. Reassessment (After D, now does B = A?)

This methodology is identical to the medical audit methodology advocated by the Joint Commission on Accreditation of Hospitals in its TAP and PEP programs. The Joint Commission workbooks and the forms provided in these workbooks can be utilized by the long term care facility for this retrospective audit. A summary of the methodology follows.

Step A, Criteria Development

The review team develops *outcome* criteria (goals or expectations for the status of the patient at the end of both the skilled nursing and intermediate levels of care) for specific diseases or problems frequently cared for in the nursing home or other long term care facility. Examples of such diseases are stroke, hip fractures, senility, etc. Criteria should be developed for those specifc diseases or problems which the review team believes have priority because of frequency of admission, high mortality or morbidity rates, or problems which in their opinion have the greatest potential for improved quality of care through continuing education programs.

Step B, Description of Performance

A pattern display of actual practice will be provided to the review team. Pattern displays will be developed by medical record personnel from data abstracted from the medical record of all patients treated over a specific time period for each disease or problem for which criteria have been developed.

Step C, Evaluation

The review team will evalute actual practice as compared with criteria to identify problem areas needing further study or correction. Evaluation will be made as to whether suboptimal care is due to performance of personnel or organization of care in the nursing home. Appropriate recommendations will be made for organizational changes or for inservice educational programs to improve the knowledge, skills, or attitude of personnel thought to be the cause of suboptimal care. Such evaluation may require an in-depth process audit to determine the reasons for suboptimal nursing care. Phaneuf, Qualpac, or Slater Scale test instruments could be recommended to the nursing staff to be used in these instances.

Step D, Corrective Action

Recommendations for appropriate corrective action will be made in writing to the nursing home administrator or the medical director of the long term care facility.

Step E, Reassessment

The review team will periodically reevaluate to determine whether the corrective action has been appropriate, as revealed by improved outcomes of the next audit. Once criteria for a specific disease or problem have been developed, medical records personnel will abstract each discharged patient's chart according to the specific criteria that have been developed, and displays will be prepared for the review team according to the number of cases which the team believes will identify an accurate pattern of care provided by the nursing home. In this way continuous profiles of care patterns will be available to the review team for continuing evaluation.

Most experts now agree that the evaluation of patterns of care is the only reliable way to measure quality. As stated in chapter 4, quality usually cannot be accurately measured on a case-by-case basis because of the number of variables not only in each patient, but in each patient's reaction to a specific disease process. Only as large numbers of cases are evaluated does a pattern of care emerge which compensates for any extremes in variation seen in individual cases. Thus, reliable profiles of individual practitioners' patterns of care or patterns of care rendered within a particular institution are developed. These profiles are also used to develop regional norms from which standards of care can be developed.

Profiles are perhaps the only reliable data that can be used in monitoring quality of care by external agencies such as PSROs. Public Law 92-603 specifically describes that monitoring of care by PSROs will be based upon such profiles. Current PSRO manuals, however, do not at this point describe these profiles except in the area of utilization review. Here the Uniform Discharge Data Set has been augmented by collecting uniform data on the utilization review process; to this point no outcome profiles have been described.

Profiles of care based on measurement by outcome criteria will eventually be the ultimate mechanism for evaluating the quality of care. It would be enlightened self-interest for providers of health care to begin the collection of four specific outcome criteria. For specific diseases or problems, the following outcomes could provide for true evaluation of quality of care. If data were collected on mortality rates, morbidity rates, efficiency of care as measured by length of stay, and cost of care as measured by total charges, then meaningful data could be collected which would provide for the simultaneous evaluation of both cost and quality. For example, institutions might justify a profile of care for a specific disease or problem in which they had an increased length of stay or a higher charge if they could show that this resulted in lower morbidity or mortality rates. If it can be shown that decreased mortality and morbidity rates can be attained only by a longer length of stay and an increase in the cost of care, then such data would be of inestimable value in documenting the necessity for improved reimbursement levels for long term care.

The historic goal of all health professions has been to improve the quality of care and the quality of life through the appropriate and wise use of the healing arts. The scientific breakthroughs of the last half century have drastically enlarged this armamentarium. Most modalities of care used today were unknown 50 years ago. The knowledge and special skills of a myriad of allied health professionals are now required to provide optimal health care, even in long term, chronic, and restorative care.

The rapid escalation in the cost of care has been due primarily to this increased armamentarium and the absolute numbers and the higher wages required for these highly skilled health care professionals. On the other hand, third party purchasers of care appear to have ample data to substantiate their claims that much of the increasing cost of care is due to inappropriate utilization of these resources, particularly of higher, more costly levels of care when equal quality of care could be provided at a less expensive, lower level (e.g., institutionalization of a patient when he could be equally well cared for on an ambulatory care basis). Unfortunately, third party purchasers of care have insured for those health care benefits only where their exposure could be estimated on an actuarily sound basis. These benefits have usually been those of higher cost and higher sophistication, and, unfortunately, consumers and providers alike have been encouraged to use those benefits covered in the various insurance programs. Third party purchasers of care have instituted utilization review programs to control overutilization and, consequently, reduce the cost of care. Providers have countered with quality assurance programs to assure that the cost containment programs of third party purchasers do not interfere with the quality of care. Consequently, it is imperative that quality assurance programs monitor both the cost and quality of care simultaneously. Therefore, the monitoring of the classes of outcome criteria mentioned above appears to be the logical way to monitor appropriate utilization and collect data to substantiate the need for adequate reimbursement for all care provided. The hope for the future, therefore, lies in the collection of these data through quality assurance programs. Providers of care will be able to predict accurately the cost of high quality optimal care. Such data can then be used by the American public in determining its national priorities.

The collection of these four classes of outcome criteria also provides for a mechanism to develop a new index of the cost of care. The index most commonly used today in determining the cost of care is the per diem rate. This is an invalid measurement, because it does not consider the patient mix in various types of health care facilities. Reimbursement in long term care is also made on the basis of per diem reimbursement rates—again showing no correlation with patient mix or the needs of individual patients. Collection of these four classes of outcome data will provide for the development of normative case rates for various diseases or problems. This would be a much more rational index of the cost of care and provide a much more rational basis for reimbursement.

In chapter 7 another mechanism that could result in a more rational reimbursement formula is also described. This is the use of a patient classification for longer term care. In the assessment step of the nursing process, it is possible to provide for a rational patient classification. By assigning weights to the various elements in this classification system, it is easy to identify the patient who requires a greater intensity of nursing care. It appears logical that this could be the basis for a more rational reimbursment mechanism.

Chapter 7

Documentation of Accountability: All About Medical Records

Medical records are used to document the care provided to an individual patient within a health care facility. Medical records serve many purposes. For example, they are necessary for medical-legal reasons and are required by external accrediting and licensing bodies. We are discussing them here because of the particular function they serve in the application of the nursing process to the care of the individual patient. As such, they become tools to aid the nurse. These tools are medical record forms. Forms permit a uniformity in the documentation of patient care. Since several nurses and other health professionals will provide care for an individual patient, uniformity makes the medical record a more easily used document which serves as a means of communication among the members of the health care team providing care to an individual patient. If data are recorded in a uniform way, they can be more easily compiled for statistical reporting and evaluation.

Forms are used in the quality assurance program to promote an orderly and rational application for the nursing process in its implementation. At first glance, the forms may appear to be complicated and cumbersome and to require too much time to complete. However, each form is designed to identify a specific essential step in the application of the nursing process. The discipline required in completing each form will lead to the development of an orderly thinking process as the nurse assesses, plans, implements, and evaluates the nursing care plan for each patient. Repetitive use of these forms will, therefore, reinforce this mental process and result in the desired goal for this entire program, namely, a change to a goal- and problem-oriented approach to nursing care.

Assessment

Medical record forms help the nurse to collect data necessary to make a nursing assessment of the patient. Forms prompt the nurse to collect all data necessary to make good judgments; they act as a reminder not to omit factors that could have an impact on the quality of care provided.

The forms used in the initial nursing assessment include the physician's care plan, the nursing history, nursing physical, and patient classification forms. Examples of these forms, those actually used in a nursing home, are included in Part II of this book. It will be noted that the data collected on the first three of these forms will be summarized on the fourth form, the patient classification. These elements of data have been adopted from a Department of Health, Education, and Welfare publication, # HRA 74-3107, *Patient Classification for Long Term Care*. This basic patient classification system will probably eventually be widely used throughout the long term care field. We have arbitrarily assigned weights to certain items of these data so that a quantitative rating of each patient can be obtained.

Planning

The forms used in the planning process are designed to help the nurse identify the patient's problems from the data collected in the assessment process, and to identify necessary nursing actions related to these problems. They identify the logical steps to the development of the nursing care plan for each patient. They also document the judgments made by the nurse in generating the nursing care plan. The forms include the Problem List and the Nursing Actions for each identified problem.

Implementation

Forms are used in the implementation process to aid in the application of the nursing care plan to the daily care of the patient. The nursing actions identified in the nursing care plan are transferred to the nursing action order cards to facilitate the carrying out of specific tasks and procedures by the appropriate nursing personnel.

Documentation of the care given by nursing attendants is recorded on the nursing attendants form. This form serves as a data base for the charge nurse in writing progress notes on the patient progress note form.

Evaluation

In writing progress notes, the charge nurse is required to evaluate the care given. Progress notes, therefore, document the evaluation process.

Patient Classification for Long Term Care

As stated above, the documentation of data on all these forms used in the application of the nursing process will be summarized on a patient classification form. A patient with a heavily weighted classification will require the greatest intensity of nursing care and require the greatest demand on the resources of the long term care facility. This system of a weighted quantitative patient classification will, therefore, be useful for several other functions:

A. Determination of staffing patterns

B. Assignment of beds

C. Determination and documentation of the appropriate level of care (skilled, intermediate, or custodial)

D. Used for reimbursement experiments in which charges can be related to the intensity of care required

Problem-Oriented Medical Records

Since the quality assurance program is a problem-oriented care concept, the records are problem oriented. The problem-oriented system is one in which each patient is considered a whole individual who has many separate problems which together contribute to his need for nursing home care to restore an optimal state of health. Nursing care is based upon the physician's medical care plan for his patient, including his estimate of the patient's restorative potential. The nursing care team identifies the patient's individual problems. Goals and objectives are developed for each problem, and specific nursing approaches to meet these needs become the nursing care plan for each patient. Periodic evaluation of the patient's progress is carried out by the nursing care team during the patient care conferences.

Uniform Discharge Data Set (UHDDS)

In federally funded programs (Medicare and Medicaid) patient data must be recorded and reported in a uniform way by all providers. One way in which patient data is recorded is known as the Uniform Hospital Discharge Data Set (UHDDS). The UHDDS is usually included in the patient information recorded on the face sheet of a patient's record. Since most long term care facilities will be required to record such data for their Medicare and Medicaid patients, it is suggested that the UHDDS format be adopted for all patient records. At the time of discharge, medical records personnel should assure that the UHDDS is accurate and complete in the medical record and that the attending physician has recorded the final diagnoses, both for the principal diagnosis and any secondary diagnoses.

Generation of the Nursing Care Plan

The orderly completion of forms in applying the nursing process to each patient results in a specific nursing care plan for each individual. This provides the necessary documentation to permit the concurrent nursing audit. Steps are summarized as follows.

Initial Nursing Assessment and Generation of Nursing Care Plan

1. Completion of UHDDS (front sheet of medical record)
2. Obtain physician's patient care plan.
    A. Physician's statement of *principal* diagnosis (reason for admission) and *secondary* diagnoses and/or problems (that may affect course of treatment or length of stay)
    B. Physician's statement of *goals* of institutionalization
        1. Expected immediate outcomes at end of each level of care and LOS estimate
            a. SNF - LOS
            b. ICF - LOS

2. Statement of restorative potential (degree of restoration thought possible) as related to each diagnosis and/or problem identified above
   a. Principal diagnosis
   b. Secondary diagnoses and/or problems
C. Physician's evaluation of likely courses of treatment
   1. Routine
   2. Complicated
D. Physician's estimate of discharge potential
   1. Home _____ (present living arrangement)
   2. Other institution _____
   3. Maintenance in _____ SNF _____ ICF _____ RCF
   4. Terminal care _____
E. Transfer physician's orders for tests, medications, and treatment to physician's order sheet.

3. Based on physician's patient care plan (2, above) obtain additional nursing care data, as necessary.
   A. Physiologic
   B. Socioeconomic
   C. Psychologic

4. Analyze and evaluate all data; identify and enumerate the patient's problem list and state the probable cause of each problem.

   Problem:
   1. _____ due to _____

   2. _____ due to _____

   3. _____ due to _____

   4. _____ due to _____

   etc. _____ due to _____

5. Categorize each problem as to *active* or *potential* (include potential problems that are likely to become active and should be watched for and/or prevented).

Problem	Active		Potential
	Onset (date)	Resolved (date)	date of evaluation
1._____	10/2	_____	_____
2._____	10/2	_____	_____
3._____	_____	_____	10/2
4._____	10/2	_____	_____

etc.

(This becomes the "problem list" which is placed as a separate sheet in the medical record just preceding the nursing progress notes.)

6. Develop nursing criteria for each problem for:

   A. *Immediate outcomes* (expected goals to be attained at the end of the care received at a specific level, e.g., SNF, ICF— that is, criteria for discharge from the specific level of care)

   B. *Intermediate outcomes* (expected objectives to be reached at specific intervals during the course of care in a specific level which the nurse believes will aid the patient in achieving the expected goals identified in A. above)

Set a time objective for each outcome for all active problems requiring nursing care. Set a date for reevaluating the need for nursing care for all active problems which the patient is currently handling himself in a satisfactory manner (and therefore does not require nursing support ot care). Set a date for reevaluating all identified potential problems.

Problem	Active		Potential	Immediate Outcomes (goals)	Date	Intermediate Outcomes (objectives)		Date
	Onset	Re-solved					Patient coping? (yes or no)	
1.								
2.								
3.								
4.								

etc.

7. Prescribe specific nursing action orders for each active problem requiring special nursing care to meet the identified objectives. The specificity for each order must include:

A. *What* is to be done
B. *Under what* circumstances
C. *When* it is to be done (include specific time or frequency)
D. *Who* is to do it (specific person or level of nursing personnel)
E. *Who* is to evaluate the effect, and how frequently (specific person)

Potential problems may require specific orders for prophylactic care or simply orders for documented observations; but these orders must be as specific as for active problems. Sign all nursing orders.

Note: These orders and the specific objectives column (see 6, above) are to be transferred to the appropriate part of the nursing plan Kardex.

Orders for active problems that can be handled by standard care routines need not be written out, but reference should be made to this fact. ("See standard care routine on Kardex.")

Note: These orders are checked on the appropriate part of the nursing care plan Kardex.

Specific attitudinal therapy will be prescribed for each patient on the basis of an evaluation of the patient's behavioral pattern. All personnel in the nursing home will be advised as to this care approach.

8. A patient classification form will be filled in based on the above nursing care plan. This form will document data necessary for the following purposes:

   A. Statistical and epidemiological reporting
   B. Determination of the appropriate *level* of care (SNF, ICF, custodial, etc.) for:
      1. Financial billing
      2. Third party reimbursement
         a. Utilization review committee
         b. PSRO requirements (Medicare and Medicaid)

9. A discharge plan will be initiated, if appropriate. Social Service personnel or agencies will be notified, as necessary, as soon as realistic discharge plans can be projected.

10. This entire document will remain intact within the medical record. It will be updated by appropriate changes in the problem list, nursing progress notes, and in the active Kardex on the basis of periodic reevaluation of the patient's progress.

Part II

Quality Assurance Program Implementation Manual

INTRODUCTION

Part II of this book is designed as a self-instructional manual for any individual or group of individuals (the health care team) wishing to implement a quality assurance program in a long term care facility. The Overview (chapter 8) describes both a concurrent and a retrospective review component. All other chapters in this part, however, refer to the concurrent review program. As such, Part II is an exposition of an approach to long term care which is goal and problem oriented; it is restorative nursing. The documentation permits a concurrent nursing audit of the care provided for each individual patient.

The forms used are those of the quality assurance program of the Near North Pavilion (the long term care unit) of Illinois Masonic Medical Center in Chicago, Illinois. They were designed to promote an orderly and rational application of the nursing process in its implementation. At first glance the forms may appear to be complicated and cumbersome and to require too much time to complete. However, each form is designed to identify a specific essential step in the application of the nursing process. The discipline required in completing each form will lead the user to develop an orderly thinking process while assessing, planning, implementing, and evaluating the nursing care plan for each patient. Repetitive use of these forms will, therefore, reinforce this mental process and will result in the desired goal for this entire program, namely, a change in nursing philosophy to a goal- and problem-oriented approach to nursing care. For nurses who are familiar with the process of writing a nursing care plan, this text alone should be adequate for learning the methodology of the Quality Assurance Program. For nurses who have not had the opportunity to develop these planning skills, a textbook is recommended for parallel study with chapter 12: *A Systematic Approach to the Nursing Care Plan* by Marlene Glover Mayers (New York: Appleton-Century-Crofts, Inc., 1972).

Chapter 8

Quality Assurance Program:
An Overview

MASTER PLAN FOR QUALITY ASSURANCE PROGRAMS

The primary goal of the IMMC Near North Pavilion is excellence in nursing home care; the institution is committed to providing the highest quality of care. This goal overrides all other objectives, because it is the basic philosophy of IMMC that if this goal is attained, all other objectives can be met. To attain this goal, a mechanism must be developed to evaluate continually the quality of care being provided so that any deficiencies can be identified and corrected. The mechanism chosen to accomplish this is a quality assurance program for nursing care (qap/nc).

In the past, we have placed our reliance on so-called *structure* measurements as an assurance of quality. These structure measurements have included the credentials of personnel, the licensure of personnel, licensure of homes by appropriate state authorities, approvals for government programs of Medicare and Medicaid, and the Joint Commission on Accreditation of Hospitals' program of accreditation for nursing homes. We are now moving to add measurements of performance to these structure measurements. These new measurement tools are known as *process* and *outcome* measurements. They will be utilized in our new program, as we believe they will permit us better to evaluate the quality of the care we provide.

Our quality assurance program is a management system based on management by objectives, which actively involves all members of the professional team responsible for patient care in each home. The methodology consists of five basic steps:

Goal setting

The patient care team sets goals for the individual patient, the unit, or the entire institution. These goals are further developed into specific objectives as steps to attain the goal. This step also includes the development of specific criteria which will be used to measure quality of care; that is, they will be yardsticks used to determine whether or not goals and objectives are being reached.

Description of performance

Using the medical record or other documentation of performance, the care provided will be measured by the criteria developed in the goal setting step. For retrospective review, medical record personnel will abstract each medical record at the time of discharge to show conformance or nonconformance to each criterion as documented in the medical record. (If care is not documented, we must assume that it was not provided.)

Evaluation

The patient care team as a group of peers will evaluate all care that does not meet the criteria which the group had set for itself. This will identify problem areas and also permit evaluation as to whether or not the goals and objectives were set too high or too low. If problems are identified, the group will determine the cause of the problem. Specifically, they will identify the cause of suboptimal care as due to deficiencies in performance of personnel or organizational barriers to high quality care. If performance of personnel is determined to be the cause, they will attempt to determine whether this is due to a deficit in knowledge, skills, or attitude. The group will then make appropriate recommendations to correct all deficiencies by correcting the cause.

Corrective action

If the group determines that problems exist and performance is suboptimal, then they will determine appropriate corrective action to improve quality of care. This is not to be considered a punitive program. We believe most personnel will respond better to a positive incentive rather than a negative incentive. Therefore, the primary mechanism to bring about change will be an inservice education program designed to improve the individual professional's knowledge, skill, or attitude. It will be the responsibility of the nursing home administrator to make the organizational changes which the peer group believes are necessary constantly to improve quality of care.

Reassessment

After the appropriate corrective action has been taken, care will be reassessed by repeating the above steps. In this way we will develop a systematic approach to constantly improving the quality of care.

The quality assurance program has two aspects: one emphasizes the care of the individual patient; the other emphasizes the pattern of care rendered by the institution to all patients with the same disease entity or problem. The first aspect is a concurrent program which is carried out while the patient is receiving care. It provides concurrent patient care evaluation by the use of goal- (or problem-) oriented nursing care and incorporates concurrent utilization review. The second aspect is carried out retrospectively (although it may include some patients still institutionalized) by periodic evaluation of the results obtained (outcomes) by analysis of the patterns of care provided all patients with the same problems or disease entities.

CONCURRENT REVIEW PROGRAM

The concurrent review program is based on a philosophy of goal-oriented nursing care. Patient care evaluation, therefore, becomes part of the day-to-day care of the patient. This type of nursing care is also problem oriented. Each patient is considered a whole individual who has many separate problems which together contribute to his need for nursing home care to restore an optimal state of health. Nursing care is based upon the physician's medical care plan for his patient, including his estimate of the patient's restorative potential. The nursing care team identifies the patient's individual problems. Goals and objectives are then developed for each problem, and specific nursing approaches to meet these goals and objectives are then identified. This results in a nursing care plan for each patient. Periodic evaluation of the patient's progress is then carried out by the nursing care team. His progress or lack of progress in meeting the specific goals and objectives in a timely manner is evaluated. Problems which interfere with achieving each objective are identified, and appropriate change in the nursing care approach is then made, better to meet the goals and objectives. This results in a dynamic nursing care plan which is always current, as it is based upon this continuing evaluation of the patient's progress.

Procedure

The nursing home will insist that a physician-generated patient care plan for each patient be documented at the time of admission and/or transfer. Patients should not be accepted in transfer unless this documentation precedes or accompanies the admission to the institution.

The director of nursing is responsible for the completion of a specific nursing care assessment of the patient at the time of admission or as soon as possible within the first 24 hours of admission to the institution. (See subsequent chapter 11 entitled Nursing Assessment.) Such assessment should follow the medical care plan for each individual patient. The director of nursing may delegate this task to an RN charge nurse.

The nursing care plan is problem oriented and written.

1. Each of the patient's problems should be identified and numbered.

2. Goals should be developed for each problem, considering the patient's restorative potential. A time estimate should also be made for obtaining each goal.

3. Specific nursing approaches to meet each goal for each problem should be identified. This should include specific tasks and procedure to be performed by other nursing personnel to help the patient reach this goal.

Periodic evaluation of the patient's progress should be documented as the patient's progress notes. This will be the responsibility of the charge nurse in each unit. Frequency of such documentation will depend upon the intensity of illness or care for the patient's specific problems, and as required by requirements for Medicare and Medicaid. All documentation should refer to the numbered problems listed in the nursing care plan. (A problem list should appear as a separate sheet preceding all progress notes. See subsequent discussion of the problem list.) Each progress note should contain the following information:

1. Subjective patient complaints and/or comments related to the problem.

2. Objective observations, by the nurse, related to the problem.

3. Assessment of the patient's new status at this time in relation to the original goal.

4. Plan for continued treatment. A specific notation should be made of a change or a continuation of the nursing care plan for this particular problem.

Note: You will notice that all progress notes, therefore, follow the format of the acronym SOAP. This acronym will remind each nurse of the necessity of addressing each of these items in each progress note.

In addition to the periodic evaluation of the patient's progress by the charge nurse, the patient's total care will be periodically evaluated by the entire patient care team—director of nurses, charge nurse, LPNs, and nurse's aides. These conferences should also be attended by other nurse specialists and other allied health professionals directly involved in the care of the patient, such as the social worker, physical therapists, etc. In this way, each patient's care would be evaluated in this inservice type educational format at least every six weeks. These patient care conferences are basically nursing care conferences, but the institution's medical director and the patient's attending physician should be encouraged to attend. These patient care conferences should also result in a statement of the nursing staff's estimate as to the patient's continued need for a specific level of care. Such estimation will be of great value to the utilization review committee in carrying out its functions.

RETROSPECTIVE REVIEW PROGRAM

The retrospective review program is complementary to the concurrent review program, which has its primary emphasis on nursing care evaluation; this program will emphasize total patient care evaluation. The review team will include physicians as well as nursing and administration. Conduct of this program will be the primary responsibility of the medical director of the nursing home. The program is designed to review the quality of care of all patients admitted to the institution. It is also designed to satisfy the opportunity available under § 1155(e) of the PSRO Amendments to Public Law 92-603, that is, permit the institution to qualify for a delegated review function by the local PSRO for its Medicare and Medicaid patients. This will probably require the addition of physicians approved by the local PSRO for participation in this program.

The methodology described at the beginning of the chapter will be utilized. The methodology will be adapted as follows by the review team:

1. Develop outcome criteria (goals or expectations for the status of the patient at the end of both the skilled nursing and intermediate levels of care for specific diseases or problems frequently cared for in the nursing home (stroke, hip fracture, senility, etc.).

2. A pattern display of actual practice will be provided to the review team. Pattern display will be developed by medical record personnel from data abstracted from the medical records of all patients treated over a specific time period for each disease or problem for which criteria have been developed.

3. The review team will evaluate actual practice as compared with criteria to identify problem areas needing further study or correction. Evaluation will be made as to whether suboptimal care is due to performance of personnel or organization of care in the nursing home. Appropriate recommendations will be made for organizational changes or for inservice educational programs to improve the knowledge, skills, or attitude of personnel thought to be the cause of suboptimal care. Such evaluation may require a more in-depth process audit to determine the

reason for suboptimal nursing care. Phaneuf, Qualpac, or Slater Scale test instruments could be recommended to the nursing staff to be used in these instances.

4. Recommendations for appropriate corrective action will be made in writing to the nursing home administrator by the medical director.

5. The review team will periodically reevaluate to determine if the corrective action has been appropriate, as revealed by improved outcomes of the next audit. Once criteria for a specific disease or problem have been developed, medical record personnel will abstract each discharged patient's chart according to the specific criteria that have been developed. Displays will be prepared for the review team according to the number of cases which the team believes will identify an accurate pattern of care provided by the nursing home. In this way, continuous profiles of care patterns will be available to the review team for continuing evaluation.

Chapter 9

The Nursing Process

There are two basic tenets which describe the uniqueness of nursing home care as compared to hospital care.

1. Nursing home care places a greater emphasis on nursing care than physician care.
2. Nursing home care is usually classified as long term care with an emphasis on restorative care and/or maintenance and support of the patient.

The quality of nursing care is of major import since it is the predominant health discipline responsible for patient care within the nursing home setting. Nurses exercise greater independence in making patient care judgments. Nurses also possess primary responsibility for the supervision and coordination of the total patient care administered.

The patient in a nursing home is one whose illness has reached medical stability and is beyond the need for acute care provided in the hospital. He now requires assistance to return to his normal state of health or prepare to live with the long term effects of his illness. So the emphasis in the nursing home is on restorative nursing care which can be characterized as wellness oriented. One must identify the positive aspects of health which the patient has maintained and strive to restore the potential which remains. In this context Henderson's definition acquires meaningful dimension and delivers great impact on the nursing practice within a nursing home. It states that:

> The unique function of the nurse is to assist the individual, sick or well, in the performance of those ac-

tivities contributing to health or its recovery (or to peaceful death) that he would perform unaided if he had the necessary strength, will, or knowledge... and to do this in such a way as to help him gain independence as rapidly as possible.[1]

Thus, nursing is a health-oriented discipline which shares goals and functions with other health professions, and, at the same time, possesses unique goals and functions in administering patient care.

Nurses fulfill their unique function through a goal-directed, patient-centered, deliberative process,[2] the components of which, in sequence, are:

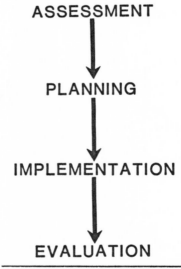

ASSESSMENT

PLANNING

IMPLEMENTATION

EVALUATION

In practice situations these four components seldom completely separate into discrete entities which neatly follow each other without overlap. Patient care evaluation as part of the day-to-day care of the patient connotes reassessment and replanning. His progress or lack of progress in meeting the specific goals and objectives in a timely manner is evaluated. Problems are identified which interfere with achieving each objective, and appropriate change in the nursing care approach is then made, better to meet the goals and objectives. This results in a dynamic nursing care plan which is always current in its implementation. Nevertheless, there is a definite directional flow which is crucial to practice because sound, effective function in any single phase requires the solid foundation of the preceding phases.

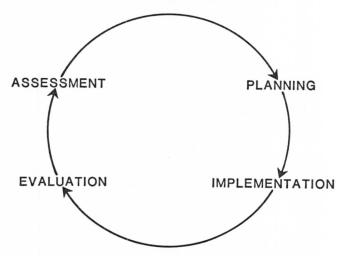

With this in mind, it is pertinent to review the components of the nursing process. It is these elements among others which form the base at which a quality assurance program is directed. The following pages delineate the characteristics of the major components of nursing process and describe some of the behaviors of the nurse as she/he moves through the systematic process.

Assessment

The practitioner:

- Obtains information through observation, interviews, analysis of records and use of vital data
- Observes, explores, and evaluates the physical and psychosocial condition of the individual and his reaction to the impact of disease and therapy on his relationships with people, work, and life-style
- Identifies age, sex, culture, economic status, and environment as factors which influence the incidence or prevalence and expression of health problems

- Identifies problems and determines nursing care needs
- Determines the urgency and complexity of the need
- Assesses the ability and readiness of individuals and families to recognize and meet their own nursing care needs
- Identifies the availability and appropriateness of resources

Implementation

The practitioner initiates nursing measures using cognitive, affective, and psychomotor skills to promote return to health, to prevent complications, and to minimize disabilities by:

- Helping recipients to make optimum use of available resources and health facilities
- Helping recipients assume responsibility for providing and arranging care and guiding them toward self-help
- Helping recipients to understand implications of the diagnosis and recommending treatment consistent with their readiness, in collaboration with the physician
- Helping recipients to utilize their capabilities and make the best possible adjustment to their limitations
- Promoting and maintaining a safe environment
- Communicating with other professional workers regarding recipients and referring pertinent information to the appropriate service or agency
- Participating in conferences with other disciplines to coordinate services
- Implementing therapeutic nursing treatments
- Interpreting and implementing medical treatments
- Reporting and recording pertinent information
- Being an advocate of the recipient
- Teaching recipients in relation to their health needs
- Providing for or actively encouraging others in the community to provide for group instruction related to health
- Applying pertinent research findings to nursing practice

Planning

The practitioner:

- Designs a nursing care plan *with* the recipient for meeting his nursing needs, *for* the recipient when he lacks the necessary resources to participate, and *with* other health professionals for meeting his total needs for health care which is appropriate and continuous
- Establishes objectives and priorities of nursing care based on needs of the recipient in relation to short and long term goals

Evaluation

The practitioner:

- Evaluates the effectiveness of nursing care to the recipient in relation to stated objectives, outcomes of care, and proven standards of care
- Assesses relationship of nursing care to the total care given by all health personnel

It is expected that these components of the nursing process are not new to every nurse. However, concentration and effort is necessary for their proper application. In order to facilitate the application of the nursing process, IMMC has developed "tools" to aid their nurses to do this in an orderly, rational, and uniform manner. These "tools" are medical record forms.

Notes

1. Virginia Henderson, *The Nature of Nursing* (New York: The Macmillan Company, 1966), p. 15.
2. Ernestine Wiedenbach, *Clinical Nursing: A Helping Art* (New York: Springer Publishing Company, Inc., 1964), p. 23.

Chapter 10

The Physician's Patient Care Plan

A physician-generated patient care plan for each patient is to precede or accompany the patient on admission to the nursing home.

A. Principal and Secondary Diagnoses: Conforms to International Classification of Diseases—U.S. Department of Health, Education, and Welfare (ICDA-8)

B. Goals for Restoration/Rehabilitation: Expected immediate outcomes at the end of a level of care in the nursing home

C. Degree of Restoration Anticipated: Statement of restorative potential as related to each diagnosis and/or problem identified

D. Length of Stay: Estimate

E. Discharge Plans: Estimate of discharge potential

F. Current Treatment Plans: Physician's orders for tests, medications, and treatments—transfer to Physician's Order Sheet

Note: Admission and/or transfer of the patient to the nursing home must be based upon this documentation (for patients whose care is to be reimbursed by federal health care programs [Titles V, XVIII, and XIX]). The preadmission evaluation of the patient must be done according to local PSRO guidelines.

Risk Factors Measurement and Medically Defined Conditions

Several factors in long term care contribute to the relevancy of compiling the data on this record. The multiplicity of diagnoses, chronic illness, and hidden or potential medical problems are pertinent items which affect the health characteristics of the patient with long term illness. Identifying such information will enhance the physician's ability to predict excessive disability and the nurse's ability to provide comprehensive care.

NEAR NORTH PAVILION, ILLINOIS MASONIC MEDICAL CENTER

REQUEST FOR ADMISSION

On or About _____

_____
　　　Patient's Name

_____
　　　Current Place of Residence

If institutionalized, please attach interfacility transfer form and a copy of history, physical examination, and discharge summary.

PHYSICIAN's CARE PLAN

Current Diagnoses	Goals for Restoration/ Rehabilitation	Degree of Restoration Anticipated

Principal

_____

Secondary

_____
_____
_____
_____

Anticipated length of stay in SNF_____

Discharge Plans:　　Home _____　　　　Other Institution _____

　　　　　　　　　Maintenance in SNF _____　　Terminal Care _____
　　　　　　　　　　　　　　ICF_____

　　　　　　　　　Other (specify)_____

Current Treatment Plans: (Outline care to be initiated in the SNF.)

_____
_____
_____
_____
_____

　　　　　　　　　　　　　_____M.D.

RISK FACTORS MEASUREMENT (Specify the readings and dates in the spaces provided below.)

	Readings	Date		Readings	Date
Height			Blood Choles.		
Weight			BUN		
Blood Pressure			Albuminurea		

CIGARETTE SMOKING (Check one and complete as applicable.)

_____ never smoked   _____ ex-smoker   _____ present smoker   _____ Number per day/present

MEDICALLY DEFINED CONDITIONS: (Check either No or Yes column for each condition listed currently present. Also specify as indicated the information for each condition in the last two columns below whether or not currently present.)

Currently present?	No	Yes	Type/Location	Duration (yr./mo.)
Alcoholism			consumption/day _____ cirrhosis _____	
Anemia			Aplastic _____ B-12 _____ Folic acid _____ Sickle cell _____ Iron (Hg < 10 mg) _____	
Angina/MI			Angina _____ MI _____	
Arthritis			Osteo _____ Joint _____ Rheumatoid _____	
Cardiac arrhythmia			At.Fib _____ BBBlock L_____ R_____ HB_____ Complete _____ Incomplete _____	
Congest. Ht. Failure			Medication Diet	
Decub. ulcers			Site Size	
Diabetes mellitus			Insulin _____ - _____ - _____ dosage Other Diet	
Drug abuse			Specify drugs	
Hypertension			B.P. _____/_____ Therapy	
Malignancy			Site Metastasis _____ Arrested _____	
Mental Illness			Psychosis _____ Anxiety _____ Depression _____	
Neuro. disorders			Specify	
Respir. disease (chr.)			Asthma _____ Bronchitis _____ Emphysema _____	

Chapter 11

Nursing Assessment

Assessment, as the first major component of the nursing process, is the step in which we gather information we need about the patient's health status and his pattern of daily living. We then use the data to formulate decisions about the patient's needs and problems. Just how important is nursing assessment? Weed's comments about data gathering in medical practice have equal validity for data gathering in nursing practice:

> Failure to define the initial data base is like playing football with a different number of men each time on a field of no definite length. Individual plays can be perfected, but their value is unclear because their context is not constant and complete. That is, an incomplete medical exploration of the patient, which, moreover may be incomplete in infinitely variable ways from patient to patient, damages the physician's ability both to determine what it is he ought to do and then to assess the quality of what he actually has done.[1]

It is helpful to use a uniform format for the collecting and recording of data. Such instruments help us to focus, clarify, and organize our information in a manner which makes it logical and easily retrievable. IMMC has, therefore, developed special forms to be used for the collection and recording of data in the assessment process.

There is, however, a cautionary note which needs to be registered here. The most important assessment tool a nurse possesses is a head, not pieces of paper! Data gathering tools are only instruments in the process, and the best nursing history forms are meaningless unless the content of the assessment reflects the nurse's ability to:

A. recognize the patient's problems,

B. search additional information that explains the cause of the problems, and

C. establish rapport and elicit information from the patient.

The content of nursing assessment as documented in IMMC forms is composed of many basic elements. It considers the special needs, characteristics, and typical problems of the patients we serve in this particular setting. For example, the collecting of detailed information about a person's recreational preferences assumes far more significance when he is entering a nursing home than when he is being admitted to an acute care hospital.

Procedure

The director of nursing is responsible for the completion of an Initial Patient Care Assessment and Nursing Care Evaluation at the time of admission to the institution.* Such evaluation should follow the physician's care plan for the patient and result in an individualized nursing care plan. The comprehensive assessment should be completed as soon as possible. The director of nursing may delegate the task of assessment to another RN.

Let us now look to the Nursing History forms and their content. The form itself is displayed on the left hand side of the manual. Additional explanation and/or relevant comments are displayed on the facing page. The latter is meant to serve as a stimulus when considering each factor. Use the form to record only the information requested. Additional comments and observations should be recorded on a separate sheet. The forms which have been adopted for use are published in *Patient Classification for*

---

*Federal programs require preadmission evaluation.

Long-Term Care: DHEW Publication number HRA 74-3107. As one completes the Nursing History forms, it will be evident that additional space is necessary to document all the acquired information. Additional sheets may be appended to these forms for the supplementary data.

NEAR NORTH PAVILION, ILLINOIS MASONIC MEDICAL CENTER
NURSING HISTORY

Date and Time of Evaluation _____ AM / /
PM _____
Mo. Day Yr.

Date of Admission (or anticipated) ___/___/___
Mo. Day Yr.

Informant _____
Patient or Other (Relationship)

SOCIO-DEMOGRAPHIC DATA

Religious Preference: _____ none   _____ Jewish   _____ other (specify)
                        _____ Catholic   _____ Protestant   _____

Race: _____ White   _____ Amer. Indian   _____ Chinese   _____ other (specify)
         _____ Black   _____ Japanese   _____ Filipino   _____

Patient Location   *Residential*   *Health Care Facility*
(present)
                    _____ private residence   _____ domicillary/personal care
                    _____ rented room (comm.)   _____ intermediate care
                    _____ apartment   _____ nursing home
                                                       _____ extended care
Site of evaluation if different   _____ chronic dis./rehab. hosp.
                                                       _____ mental hospital
_____   _____ other specialty hospital
                                                       _____ short term acute hosp.

Length of time   If residential   If Health Care Facility
at Location   Specify date:
                   _____   This admission _____
                   yrs./mos.   First admission _____

Living Arrangements   _____ own home   _____ alone
(ck. those that   _____ another's home   _____ with spouse
apply)   _____ paying   _____ with other, who _____
                       _____ not paying   _____ health related facil.
                       _____ rented room   _____(type)

Living Children — specify by number: sons _____   daughters _____

Education   _____ college grad. (beyond baccalaureate)   _____ high school diploma
             _____ undergrad. coll./degree   _____ trade, tech., voc. school
             _____ some undergrad./no degree   with h.s. diploma
             _____ trade, tech., voc. school   _____ 9-11 grades completed
                    no h.s. diploma   _____ 8 grades completed
             _____ no school   _____ fewer than 8 grades completed

Usual Occupation   Specify   or ck. _____ military   _____ housewife
                    _____   _____ never employed

See instructions — facing page

Component	*Additional Content that may be Recorded*
Religious Preference	1. Attendance at religious services 2. Name of clergyman/visitation 3. Date of last rites 4. Religious food habits 5. Church affiliation 6. Bible reading pattern/prayer pattern 7. 8.
Race-Ethnic Group	1. Cultural traditions/background 2. Languages spoken 3.
Patient Location (refers to place patient resided immediately before admission to a nursing home)	1. Name of facility 2. Reason of stay at this facility 3. Reason for transfer to nursing home 4.
Length of Stay at above Location	1. Attitude regarding stay 2.
Living Arrangements (refers to *usual* living arrangements before onset of present illness)	1. Health of spouse or other 2. One-story, two-story dwelling 3. Description of a typical day 4.
Living children	1. Names and location 2. Visits of relations 3. Grandchildren 4. Relatives: relationship and location 5.
Education	1. Ability to learn; accept directions 2. General intelligence 3.
Usual Occupation	1. Length of service 2. Type of setting as factory, office 3.

SOCIO-DEMOGRAPHIC DATA (cont.)

Employment Status   _____ employed   _____ working, hrs/wk _____
     _____ rec. pay   _____ inside home/facility
     _____ retired   _____ outside home/facility
     _____ unemployed   _____ receiving pension
     _____ never in labor market

Family Income   _____ less than $3,000   _____ $7,000-$9,999
(ck. one)   _____ $3,000-$4,999   _____ $10,000-$14,999
     _____ $5,000-$6,999   _____ $15,000 +

Health Care   _____ None   List other health insurance patient has.
Coverage   _____ Medicare   (Specify below.)
     _____ Medicaid   _____
     _____ Workmen's comp.   _____

Hobbies/special interests _____

_____

Psychological Data _____

For oriented patients, describe the patient's adjustment to illness and new environment:

_____

_____

Describe patient's goals or objectives _____
(for care in nursing home)_____

_____

_____

_____

Functioning Status _____

Mode of admission   _____ ambulatory   _____ w/c   _____ stretcher   _____ other

General physical condition:

_____

_____

Allergies:

_____

_____

See instructions — facing page

Component	*Additional Content that may be Recorded*
Employment Status	1. Feelings about status 2. Adjustment to status 3. 4.
Family Income	1. Source of income: spouse, self 2.
Health Care Coverage	1. Source of revenue for institutionalization 2. Term for benefits 3. Restrictions to benefits 4.
Hobbies/Special Interests	1. Type of reading: newspaper, books 2. Games as chess, checkers, cribbage, cards 3. Crafts as knitting, needlepoint 4. Music—type for listening 5. Radio/TV programs 6.
Psychological Data	1. Feelings about illness and admission 2. Patient's part in decision to enter facility 3. Understanding of illness 4. Reaction to admission 5.
Patient's Goals/Objectives	1. What does he expect from stay? 2. Does he expect to return home? 3. How long does he expect to stay? 4.
Functioning Status Mode of Admission	1. Accompanied by: 2. 3.
General Physical Condition	1. Good, fair, poor 2. 3.
Allergies	1. Medications 2. Foods 3. Dust, feathers, etc. 4. Pollen 5.

NEAR NORTH PAVILION, ILLINOIS MASONIC MEDICAL CENTER
NURSING HISTORY (Continued)

FUNCTIONAL ASSESSMENT

Mobility Level
Goes outside facility
_____ w/o help
_____ with help, describe

Moves about facility
_____ w/o help
_____ with help, describe
_____

Confined
_____ chair
_____ bed

Describe devices used _____

Transferring
Transfers
_____ w/o help $\boxed{0}$
_____ with help, describe $\boxed{4}$

Does not Transfer
_____ done by others $\boxed{16}$
_____ bedfast

Describe devices used

Walking
Walks
_____ w/o help $\boxed{0}$
_____ with help, describe $\boxed{16}$

Does not Walk
_____ bedfast
_____ chairfast

Describe devices used

Wheeling
Wheels
_____ w/o help $\boxed{0}$
_____ with help, describe $\boxed{4}$

Does not wheel
_____ walks
_____ chairfast
_____ bedfast
_____ is wheeled by others $\boxed{8}$

Describe devices used

Stair Climbing
Goes up and down stairs
_____ w/o help $\boxed{0}$
_____ with help, describe $\boxed{8}$

Does not climb stairs
_____ goes up/down curb
_____ goes up/down one/two steps
_____ uses ramp for one/two steps
_____ uses elevator/chair lift

Describe devices used _____

Bathing
Bathes
_____ w/o help $\boxed{0}$
_____ with help, describe $\boxed{18}$
_____ or
_____ is bathed by others
(See next column.)

Where Bathed
_____ bed $\boxed{20}$
_____ sink $\boxed{18}$
_____ tub $\boxed{18}$
_____ shower $\boxed{18}$

Describe devices used

Dressing
Dresses
_____ w/o help $\boxed{0}$
_____ with help, describe
See 3rd column.

_____ is dressed by others $\boxed{30}$
regularly (any clothes)

Kind of Dress
_____ street clothes only $\boxed{5}$
_____ robe & PF/gown only $\boxed{5}$
_____ slippers only $\boxed{5}$
_____ shoes only $\boxed{5}$
_____ 2 or more of above $\boxed{20}$

Note: Ignore for the moment the weighted values assigned to certain elements, identified by $\boxed{\text{X}}$ these will be discussed in Chapter 15, Patient Classification.
See instructions — facing page

Component	*Additional Content that may be Recorded*
Mobility Level	1. Usual forms of exercise prior to illness and admission 2. Restrictions or limitations 3. Body alignment 4. Ability to change positions in bed 5. Exercise tolerance 6. Aberrant movements, tics, habitual movements 7. 8.
Transferring	1. Restrictions or limitations 2. Use of upper extremities 3. Coordination; dominant side 4. 5.
Walking	1. Posture Devices: 2. Gait Person 3. Weakness Walker 4. Position Sense Cane 5. Elastic Stockings 6.
Wheeling	1. Prescription Wheelchair 2. One-hand 3. Coordination 4. 5.
Stair Climbing	1. Amount of physical exertion 2. 3.
Bathing	1. Type of bathing preferred 2. Time of bathing preferred 3. Items with bath: powder, oil, lotion 4. Frequency of baths preferred 5. Shampoo 6. Shaving 7. 8.
Dressing	1. Favorite items of clothing 2. Usual style of dress 3. 4.

FUNCTIONAL ASSESSMENT (cont.)

Eating/Feeding

Eats

_____ w/o help   [0]

_____ with help, describe   [20]

_____

Describe any devices used _____

Where

_____ bed

_____ chair in room

_____ dining room

Is Fed

_____ orally by others   [45]

_____ tube fed   [45]

_____ parentally fed   [45]

Toileting

Uses Toilet Room

_____ w/o help   [0]

_____ with help, describe   [8]

_____

Describe any devices used _____

When

_____ all the time

_____ day only

_____ never

Substitutes

_____ bedpan/urinal   [8]

_____ commode   [8]

Bowel Function

_____ no problem   [0]

_____ impaction

_____ involuntary loss   [18]

_____ bowel training   [18]

Ostomy

_____ self care

_____ not self care   [18]

Describe devices used

_____

_____

Bladder Function

_____ no problem   [0]

_____ retention

_____ involuntary loss   [48]

_____ bladder training   [50]

_____ ostomy

_____ indwelling catheter [20]

_____ external device

   describe

_____ self care

_____ not self care   [20]

Describe any devices used _____

Orientation (Check one and complete as applicable.)

_____ oriented   [0]

_____ disoriented

_____ comatose   [36]

If disoriented, use the table to indicate by (x) the area(s) and frequency.

   Always [16]   or   Part-Time [8]

   Time _____

   Place _____

   Person _____

Communication of needs (Check one and complete as applicable.)

_____ verbally   [0]

_____ nonverbally, specify how _____ [4]

_____ does not communicate [8]
   (but not comatose)

See instructions — facing page

Component	*Additional Content that may be Recorded*
Eating/Feeding	1. Food/amounts eaten 2. Likes and dislikes, beliefs about food 3. Types of food eaten, fluids drunk at home 4. Usual meal times, appetite 5. Special diet restrictions 6. Snacks, fruit, etc. 7. Estimate of glasses of fluid drunk per day 8. Position and supports needed 9.
Toileting	1. Upon arising/at bedtime/meals 2. Candidate for bowel/bladder program 3.
Bowel Function (elimination of feces)	1. Regular pattern: frequency; time of day 2. Bowel sounds 3. Occurrence of constipation, diarrhea 4. Use of laxatives, enemas, antidiarrheal, medications 5. Presence of pain, bleeding 6. Abdominal distension 7. Incontinence 8. Altered route 9.
Bladder Function (elimination of urine)	1. Frequency: daytime, nighttime 2. Amount 3. Degree of urgency 4. Appearance of urine 5. Presence of pain, bleeding 6. Use of diuretics 7. Incontinence: stress, intermittant, continuous
Orientation	1. Knows own name, age 2. Knows time: year, season, month, day, hour 3. Knows places: name of nursing home, city, state 4. Recognition of other people: family, spouse, doctor, nurses 5. Any photgraphs for identification 6. Candidate for Reality Orientation 7.
Communication of Needs	1. Answers questions readily; reluctantly 2. Demanding; embarrassed 3. Non-questioning; non-talkative 4. Questioning 5. Quick/slow/unable to comprehend 6. Seeks support 7.

NEAR NORTH PAVILION, ILLINOIS MASONIC MEDICAL CENTER
NURSING HISTORY (Continued)

BEHAVIOR PATTERN

Check and complete as appropriate.

_____ appropriate behavior   ☐0   _____ once a week or less   ☐1
_____ inappropriate behavior   _____ more often than once a week   ☐2
   _____ wandering, passive ☐1   _____ able to follow instructions
   _____ abusive, aggressive ☐3
   _____ agitated   ☐2
   _____ hallucinating   ☐2
   _____ withdrawn   ☐2
   _____ depressed   ☐2

_____ THIS COLUMN TOTAL X _____ THIS COLUMN TOTAL = ☐

Narrative exposition of frequent patterns:

_____

_____

_____

_____

_____

_____

_____

_____

_____

_____

_____

_____

_____

Nursing History forms continue on next page.

IMPAIRMENTS

Sight	Type of compensation

Sight

_____ no impairment

_____ legally blind

_____ impairment, describe

_____

Type of compensation

_____ glasses

_____ contact lens

_____ large print

_____ other, describe _____

Hearing

_____ no impairment

_____ does not hear

_____ impairment, describe

_____

Type of compensation

_____ loud voices

_____ shouting

_____ hearing aid

_____ lip reading

_____ other, specify _____

Describe any devices used _____

Speech

_____ no impairment

_____ does not speak

_____ impairment, describe

_____

Type of compensation

_____ writes

_____ gestures

_____ sign language

_____ other, specify _____

Fractures and Dislocations

_____ none

_____ hip fracture

    _____ with prosthesis

    _____ with repair

_____ other fracture(s), describe

_____

_____ dislocation(s), describe

_____

_____

Joint Motion

_____ no impairment   _____ impairment, use table to specify site joint and side(s) and check column for type

---

Joint site (R, L, B)	pain/ swelling	limited mobility	immobility	instability

See instructions — facing page

Component	*Additional Content that may be Recorded*
Vision	1. Use of glasses or contact lenses: reason when worn 2. Ability to read: size of print; magnifying glass 3. Blurring 4. Eye fatigue 5. Tearing 6. Irritation 7. Use of eye drops 8. Night Light 9. Last eye examination 10. Prosthesis
Hearing	1. Unilateral or bilateral loss 2. Use of hearing aid, provisions for batteries 3. Understanding of speech 4. Need for speaker to talk loudly, talk slowly, repeat self 5. Ability to lip read 6.
Speech	1. Loudness 2. Pitch 3. Accent 4. Rate 5. Amount 6. Spontaneity 7. Stuttering or hesitancy 8. Coherence 9. Blocking 10. Circumstantiality 11. Flight of ideas 12. Mutism 13. Speech defect 14.
Fractures and Dislocations	1. Tendency to fragility 2.
Joint Motion	1. History of arthritis 2. Other causes for limitations 3. Contractures: degree of 4.

NEAR NORTH PAVILION, ILLINOIS MASONIC MEDICAL CENTER
NURSING HISTORY (Continued)

IMPAIRMENTS (cont.)

Missing Limbs

_____ none missing

_____ missing, use table to specify missing part(s) and check column for prosthesis

Missing part(s)	Rt., left, both	Prosthesis

Paralysis

_____ none
_____ paralysis, describe type and location

_____ muscular weakness, wasting or atrophy

_____

_____

Dentition

_____ no teeth missing
_____ some teeth missing
_____ edentulous
_____ special diet, describe

Type of compensation
_____ partial plate
_____ complete upper plate
_____ complete lower plate
_____ other appliances, describe

_____   _____

See instructions — facing page

Component	*Additional Content that may be Recorded*
Missing Limbs	1. Mobility adjustment due to prosthesis or the like 2. Attitude regarding loss 3.
Paralysis	1. Residual/potential 2. Physical Therapy 3.
Dentition	1. Condition of teeth, gingiva, tongue 2. Interference with capacity to eat: ability to chew, swallow, presence of pain, nausea, vomiting, anoxeria 3. Usual method of cleaning teeth (Polident, soak, brush with Pepsodent) 4. 5.

Nursing Physical

The nurse is to examine the patient physically and note the pertinent findings. This is not meant to be a duplication of the physician's physical examination; it is an opportunity for the nurse to obtain first-hand knowledge of the patient's physical condition upon admission to the nursing home. Let us proceed to review the tool IMMC has adopted for use.

NEAR NORTH PAVILION, ILLINOIS MASONIC MEDICAL CENTER
NURSING PHYSICAL

Including Review of Symptoms

Document assessments and observations of the following:

Component Observed	Additional Content that may be Recorded — Systemic Review
Vital Signs	
Blood Pressure	1. Systolic and Diastolic (R) arm ____/____
	2. Systolic and Diastolic (L) arm ____/____
Pulse	1. Quality:
	2. Rhythm:
	3. Rate:
Respiration	1. Quality:
	2. Rate:
Weight	1. Compare to normal range for height (____ in.) ____
EENT	
Eyes	1. Glaucoma, cataract
	2. Diploplia
	3. Infection
	4. Recent change
	5. *
Ears	1. Earaches
	2. Vertigo
	3. Discharge, infection
	4.
Nose	1. Sinus pain
	2. Postnasal drip
	3. Epistaxis
	4.

*Note: Additional spaces left for other positive findings.

Component Observed	*Additional Content that may be Recorded — Systemic Review*
EENT (Cont.)	
Throat	1. Toothache
	2. Bleeding, cracked lips
	3. Gums, mouth, tongue
	4. Hoarseness
	5.
Neck	1. Limitation of motion
	2.
	3.
Chest	
Lungs	1. Dyspnea
	2. Orthopnea
	3. Wheezes, rales
	4.
Heart	1. Apical-Radial Pulse _____/_____
	2. Palpitation
	3.
	4.
Breasts	1. Discharge
	2. Pain
	3. Mass
	4.
Abdomen	1. Mass
	2. Hernia (truss?)
	3.
	4.
Genitalia	1. Discharge, odor
	2. Pap smear
	3.
	4.
Rectum	1. Hemorrhoids
	2. Fecal impaction
	3.
	4.
Extremities	1. Varicose veins
	2. Thrombophlebitis
	3. Range of motion capability
	4. Joint swelling
	5.
	6.
Skin	1. Color
	2. Tone, turgor
	3. Lesions
	4. If decubiti, location and measure width and depth.

Chapter 12

Nursing Care Planning

While nursing assessment yields data about the patient's condition and leads to the determination of his needs and problems, the nursing care plan lends direction to the nursing staff via goals, objectives, and actions which result in optimum health for the patient. It is the second component of the nursing process. To supply the theory content on nursing care planning, *A Systematic Approach to the Nursing Care Plan* by Marlene Glover Mayers (Appleton-Century-Crofts, Inc., New York, 1972) is recommended.

In Mayers' text, "A Nursing care plan is an abstract of data concerning a specific patient—data which is organized in a concise and systematic manner, which facilitates overall medical and nursing goals and which clearly communicates the nature of the patient's problems and the nature of the related medical and nursing orders." [1] To put it another way, "Nursing care plan is a brief orientation to the patient and his care—a guide to patient-centered care." [2] It is patient-centered care rather than personnel-centered or disease-centered care. Information is listed about the patient, and he is given primary consideration as the aspects of his medical and his nursing care are identified. As goals and objectives of care are established and nursing interventions outlined, perhaps the one essential member is too often not involved in writing a nursing care plan—the patient himself. Before one attempts to establish goals and objectives for a specific patient, that patient should relate what his own desires are for the particular cycle of care before him.

In chapter 2, Mayers elaborates on the elements of a nursing care plan with specific examples to demonstrate its format. These elements which are adopted by IMMC in its system for nursing care planning are:

1. List of patient's problems/needs
   Cause of problem
   Active/potential problems
   Evaluation of problems
2. Goals/objectives/outcomes of patient care
3. Nursing actions/interventions

The system also incorporates the problem-oriented concept of care. The nursing care plan is problem oriented in that each of the patient's problems is identified with its cause delineated. The latter is important since it yields the reasoning and basis for decision making when determining goals. Problems are identified as Active/Actual or Potential, because high quality care focuses on preventive aspects as well as therapeutic aspects of care. Then goals are developed for each problem (expected outcomes). The patient's restorative potential must be considered as well as a time estimate for the attainment of the goal/outcome. Let us now look at each of these elements and the tools which have been developed to assist you in implementing nursing care planning.

THE PROBLEM-ORIENTED APPROACH

As you perform the patient assessment, problems are identified, listed, and numbered. The problem-oriented approach[3] is not unique for you since nurses have implemented it for quite some time in nursing care plans. However, the advent of problem-oriented records has necessitated additional insight in their application. It is essential to be skilled in the identification of all the problems a patient is experiencing in relation to his illness; this is the basis for the planning of nursing care. It leads to making appropriate decisions as to when there should be nursing intervention directed toward the solution of the problems.

An important tool is the Problem List. It is placed (as a separate sheet) in the patient record just preceding the nursing progress notes. It provides for the listing of each problem by number as it is identified; a problem is listed as "active" or "potential" in the appropriate column; dates of onset and resolution are completed when appropriate; it also records the date the problem was evaluated. This tool serves as an inventory of the problems faced by the patient. It also serves as an assisting device in monitoring the progress being made in resolution of the problems; documentation follows the progress made for each problem as outlined above.

Traditionally, nurses have had a tendency to state problems as medical diagnoses rather than conditions requiring nursing intervention. Let us use an example to explain this better. Example: A patient with the medical diagnosis of leukemia in its final stages. Leukemia is the medical diagnosis. The problem can be identified as being terminally ill. One patient need can be identified as the need to face death with dignity. Other needs might include psychological comfort, perhaps through family contact on a continuous basis; freedom from pain in order to feel in control of the circumstances; or the attention of a clergyman, depending on the patient's religious beliefs. It would be up to the nurse to assess the patient's need and decide which approaches would be relevant.

As we further discuss the identification of problems and needs, perhaps it might be helpful to understand the difference between these two terms. A *need* is a component which is necessary for life and is involved with the individual's response to his environment and to his living. A *problem,* on the other hand, arises when conflict occurs in the satisfaction of need, either because of disease or some other inadequacy in the individual's life. It is at this point that intervention is critical in order for the individual to enjoy health.

Let us consider another example for further clarification. A patient has Parkinson's Disease. Parkinson's Disease is the medical diagnosis. The physician may have prescribed medications such as L-dopa and treatments such as speech therapy, physical therapy, etc. One need which a patient has is proper nutrition. One problem which may result as a direct result of Parkinson's Disease is poor nutrition because the patient has difficulty chewing due to muscle rigidity and lack of motor ability affecting the oral and neck muscles. (Here we have included the cause of the problem.) The nursing action directed toward a solution of the problem would be to prescribe special feedings: pureed food, ground meat, protein liquid nourishment, and small, frequent meals.

An important dimension in identifying problems is to list the cause of the problem. This is important because patients may have problems which are stated the same but which have different causes. The nursing intervention will certainly be influenced by the cause and therefore the cause should be listed. Chapter 3 of Mayers provides further discussion on identifying problems. Included are specific examples typical to the long term care setting.

Also included is a discussion of handling problems with which the patient is or is not coping. It is important for the nurse to identify this situation, especially in the long term care, since the philosophy is to provide a sense of wellness in the patient; that is, to identify his ability to be independent and to intervene only when necessary. It is important that the nurses do not intervene when a patient is coping with a problem. However, when a patient is not coping, a problem exists and nursing intervention is necessary. However, it is possible that a patient may be coping but may need some unique assistance from the nursing staff in order to cope better. In this instance it would be beneficial to include such interventions which also assist the patient.

Dates for onset and resolution on the problem list are important in order to anticipate the duration of the problem as well as lend an incentive to its solution in an optimal span of time. Time span is important in assessment of a problem because it leads to the identification of stages in the path to resolution of a problem. (See Exhibit 12-1).

GOALS, OBJECTIVES AND OUTCOMES

The second essential element of the nursing care plan is that of setting objectives in order to meet the needs of the patient. This approach to patient care is an adaptation of "management by objectives" and is meant to be an integral part of IMMC's quality assurance program. It truly represents the basic philosophy of patient-centered or goal-oriented nursing care. It lends direction and purpose to one's patient care activities and enhances the possibility of successfully resolving the patient's health problems. Setting a goal is more likely to result in success than is providing routine care with no specific objective in mind.

Exhibit 12-1

NEAR NORTH PAVILION, ILLINOIS MASONIC MEDICAL CENTER
PROBLEM LIST

Problem #	Active Problem	Onset Date	Resolve Date	Potential Problem	Eval. Date

Mayers refers to goals as expected outcomes, and this ter-
minology has been adapted in the IMMC system in a further divi-
sion into immediate and intermediate outcomes. A separate form
has been devised for you to catalog the outcomes and concomitant
nursing interventions for each problem on the problem list. The
immediate outcome refers to the goal which is to be attained at
the end of the cycle of care in a particular level of care in the nursing home. (Levels of long term care are frequently identified as
skilled, intermediate, and custodial.) Intermediate outcomes are
those objectives to be reached at specific intervals during the
course of care at a particular level. They are short term objectives
which ultimately lead to the achievement of the long term or ultimate goal for that particular level of care.

It is vital to establish objectives which are specific to the patient
and his state of health. It is not sufficient to make broad general
statements, such as, "to maintain present level of health." (What
is the patient's level of health? What behavior and/or activity do
you want to maintain as part of the patient's daily life?) As one
writes objectives or expected outcomes, one should identify the
behavior which the patient and the nurse desire at the end of his
episode in the health care institution.

One might wonder what a long term expected outcome might be
within the nursing home setting, particularly if the patient will be
remaining in a nursing home setting for an indefinite period or
perhaps a lifetime (custodial level of care). In this instance, the
expected outcome will still refer to conditions and behaviors expected to be achieved or maintained as a result of the institutionalization. Once the optimal restorative potential has been
reached, then it is a matter of continuing the nursing intervention
to maintain this state of health. Be sure to study chapter 4 of
Mayers' text for further help on how to describe outcomes which
are specific to the patient and to the problem that he manifests.

Specific Nursing Actions

In order to achieve the objectives or outcomes of care for each
problem, nursing care activities are determined and prescribed in

Exhibit 12-2

NEAR NORTH PAVILION, ILLINOIS MASONIC MEDICAL CENTER
NURSING ACTIONS FOR PROBLEM NUMBER _____

(Use separate sheet for *each* problem on problem list.)

Problem _____

Date of Onset _____   Date Resolved _____

Immediate Outcome (goals)   □ Date to be accomplished/reevaluated

Intermediate Outcome (objectives)	By what date	Specific nursing action (if prn, state circumstances)	Date begin	Time/frequency	Who performs	Evaluation who/frequency

Nursing actions should be transferred to "Nursing Action Order Card" (Kardex) and noted at that time.

For patient classification—nursing action guideline used for this problem □ .

_____
Nurse's Signature/Title

Exhibit 12-3

IMMC: Nursing Actions Order Card

RESIDENT CARE PLAN

DATE	PROBLEMS AND NEEDS	DATE REVIEWED	PLAN OF APPROACH	DATE SOLVED

FEED ☐   T.P.R.   B.P.   INTAKE OUTPUT HEIGHT WT.   CLINITEST   BED BATH ☐   ASSIST ☐
ASSIST ☐   TUB ☐   SHOWER ☐

DIET:	GENERAL ☐	SOFT ☐	OTHER ☐	TREATMENTS:	TIME DUE
NOURISHMENT:					
TRANSPORTATION:	WALK ☐	WHEEL CHAIR ☐	CART ☐		
SIDE RAILS:	CONSTANTLY ☐	NIGHT ☐			
ACTIVITY & POSITION:	UP AD LIB ☐				
BEDREST ☐	BRP ☐				
CHAIR ☐	AMBULATE ☐				

100 018-1   IMMC - NEAR NORTH PAVILION   COMMUNICATION CONTINUATION CARD

DATE ORD.	ROUTINE MEDICATIONS	TIME DUE	DATE ORD.	H.S. & P.R.N. MEDICATIONS	TIME DUE

ALLERGIC TO:

DIAGNOSIS

HOSPITAL NO.   RELIGION   BIRTHDAY   SURGERY & DATE

ROOM   NAME   AGE   ADMISSION DATE   DOCTOR

the form of nursing action orders. Each order or nursing action must include:

A. What is to be done.

B. When it is to be done (time/frequency).

C. Who is to do it (level of nursing personnel).

D. Who is to evaluate the effect and how frequently.

This is where the professional nurse's unique skill is necessary. These judgments and decisions are based on the assessment and identification of the patient's problems.

There must be *nursing orders* for nursing actions in addition to the physician's medical orders. Mayers supplies in-depth instructions on how to write nursing actions in chapter 5. Several examples are provided, particularly some applicable to the long term care setting. (See Exhibit 12-2; also see Appendix B for sample nursing care plan using these forms.)

While each active problem has specific nursing action orders, the potential problems may simply necessitate orders for specific periodic observations. Some potential problems may require orders for prophylactic care (such as back care for prevention of decubiti). Dates are to be set for the initiation of the nursing care order and then the time identified for reevaluating the need for the nursing care prescribed.

All nursing action orders are to be transferred to the Nursing Actions Order Card. This card has already been in use at IMMC as a Kardex card reflecting the patient's "nursing care plan." It is meant to be readily usable for the team members as they conduct day-to-day patient care activities. It is also useful to the charge nurse in planning the assignment of personnel to patients. During patient care conferences it can be used to review and update the patient's care. (See Exhibit 12-3.)

Notes

1. Marlene Glover Mayers, *A Systematic Approach to the Nursing Care Plan* (New York: Appleton-Century-Crofts, Inc., 1972), p. 12.

2. Sister Mary Dennis Shay, ed., *The Management of Nursing Care: A Development Program for Head Nurses* (St. Louis: The Catholic Hospital Association, 1968).

3. Thora Kron, *The Management of Patient Care* (Philadelphia: W.B. Saunders Co., 1971), p. 11.

Chapter 13

Evaluation of Nursing Care

Evaluation is the next step in the nursing process. This is the step that permits the nursing process to be used as an audit process. This is where we evaluate and document the patient's response or lack of response to the nursing care plan for each of his problems.

Evaluation of the patient's response is periodically made by the nurse in charge of each patient. Evaluations are recorded in the patient's progress notes. These data are then used by the entire patient care team periodically to evaluate the nursing care plans for each of the patient's problems. Patient care conferences are held for this purpose. Based on these evaluations, new goals and objectives for each problem are set, new nursing actions written, and the cyclic process of a goal- and problem-oriented approach to nursing care is achieved.

Essential to any quality assurance program is meaningful documentation regarding the patient's health, the judgments made in assessing and evaluating his condition, and the actions or care performed on his behalf. Appropriate documentation enables continuity of care among team members. The SOAP format to be utilized in documenting the evaluation for each problem on the Nurse's Progress Notes was originally suggested by Dr. Lawrence Weed.

It represents the application of an essentially new thought process while you perform recording of the patient's care. It will take time and practice to become adept with the method, but it is well worth the effort. The data that will now be recorded will take new, meaningful form and will greatly assist you to provide a higher quality of care. (See Exhibit 13-1.)

Exhibit 13-1

NEAR NORTH PAVILION, ILLINOIS MASONIC MEDICAL CENTER
PROGRESS NOTES

DATE	NOTES ARE TO BE SIGNED BY AUTHOR
	Specific problem number (see problem list) to which each progress note is addressed should be listed.
	Follow format as outlined: Subjective complaints
	Objective observation by nurse of patient's reaction to problem or treatment
	Assessment of patient's current status in relationship to original goals/objectives
	Plan for continued treatment; change in nursing care plan

Exhibit 13-2

NEAR NORTH PAVILION, ILLINOIS MASONIC MEDICAL CENTER NURSE ATTENDANT RECORD

	Sunday			Monday			Tuesday			Wednesday			Thursday			Friday			Saturday		
	Date			Date			Date			Date			Date			Date			Date		
	B	L	D	B	L	D	B	L	D	B	L	D	B	L	D	B	L	D	B	L	D
Diet: % eaten at each meal																					
Spoon fed / Fed self	7/3	3/11	11/7	7/3	3/11	11/7	7/3	3/11	11/7	7/3	3/11	11/7	7/3	3/11	11/7	7/3	3/11	11/7	7/3	3/11	11/7
Tub / Shower / Bed																					
Mouth Care																					
Incontinent: Bowel / Bladder / Continent																					
Bed-Turned q2h / Confined-chair / Amb. w/assist. / Up & about																					
Alert / Forgetful / Confused / Uncooperative / Cooperative																					

Signature:
Day 7/3
PM 3/11
Night 11/7

B = breakfast   L = lunch   D = dinner

Exhibit 13-2 (Continued)

WEEKLY SUMMARY

Date _____

B.P. _____ P _____ R _____ Temp _____

Eating Pattern: _____

Personal Toilet (Appearance, Mouth care, Bathing, Dressing): _____

Bowel/Bladder Pattern: _____

Ambulation/Activities: _____

Rest/Sleep Pattern: _____

Interpersonal Relationships: (Environment, Other Patients, Personnel, Family) _____

RECORD OF INCIDENTS

Date	Time	Incident	Reported to	Signature

Since nurse assistants perform much of the daily, direct patient care activities, their observations and performance yield much information and influence the total patient care picture. A Nurse Attendant Record has been devised for the nursing attendant to record appropriate notes.* (See Exhibit 13-2.) The charge nurse, in turn, utilizes these records in compiling the periodic summaries on the Progress Notes.

These two forms, problem-oriented progress notes and nurse attendant record, are designed to eliminate the need for writing "nurse's notes" for each shift. Such notes are frequently meaningless and require too much time to be spent in charting. The problem-oriented progress note approach results in only meaningful nurse's notes. At first glance they appear to be requiring more documentation; in practice, however, because notes are written only when necessary, less writing is required. The nurse attendant record is also designed to eliminate shift notes. The nurse attendant who is giving the routine bedside care uses the checklist to record her activities in patient care. Specific incidents are recorded to reflect any unusual occurrence. And, if the charge nurse keeps a separate medication record book, all requirements for the traditional "shift charting" will be met through the use of these forms.

The forms provided in this chapter are designed to enable the charge nurse to document the evaluation of the patient's progress in a problem-oriented format. By evaluating the progress made toward resolving each problem separately and documenting this in the progress notes according to the SOAP format, the nurse has been forced to perform the evaluation in relation to the specific therapeutic objectives written in the nursing care plan. The written progress notes document the thinking process in this evaluation:

S = Subjective notes provide for documenting the patient's input into the evaluation. (e.g., "I feel better, but that new medicine upsets my stomach.")

---

*One of these forms is to be kept for each patient. It is to be filled out during each shift, every day of the week, and the summary section completed at week's end. It is suggested that these worksheets be kept in a looseleaf notebook at the nurses' station.

O = Objective notes record the nurse's observations. (e.g., "Since beginning the penicillin she has not eaten well; she belches frequently and her upper abdomen is distended.

Her temperature, however, has returned to normal, 99^6 F. Lungs clear.")

A = Assessment records the significance of the subjective and objective observations and their meaning in relationship to the therapeutic objective. (e.g., "The penicillin has been effective in treating her pneumonia, but is apparently causing a gastrointestinal upset. There is no skin rash or other symptoms to make me feel this is an allergic reaction.")

P = Plan records any change in nursing actions contemplated as a result of the evaluation. (e.g., "I called Doctor Jones in regard to the GI upset and communicated my thoughts in regard to penicillin as the cause. He ordered the penicillin to be given with skim milk instead of water. Will see if this helps.")

In most instances, this type of evaluation by the charge nurse (that is, writing progress notes) will be performed in relation to an objective (an intermediate outcome) rather than in relation to a goal (an immediate outcomes as these terms are defined in chapters 4 and 9).

Progress notes should be written as often as necessary to describe a change (either improvement or worsening) in the progress toward reaching an objective. They should also be written to describe no improvement if a change has been anticipated following the implementation of a nursing action or a physician's order. (In writing nursing actions, a time frame is specified when anticipated change is expected; see chapter 12.) For problems requiring a skilled level of care, progress notes are usually required daily, or even every shift. For problems requiring less acute care, progress notes should be written at least once every week. For example, a patient with six problems could require progress notes dealing with one of his problems every shift and for another, every day; but all six should be evaluated at least once a week.

It should now be obvious that a nurse performing the type of evaluation required for writing problem-oriented progress notes is actually carrying out a "mini-cycle" of the nursing process. By entering the cycle at the *evaluation* step, the nurse is forced to collect new data (S= a limited history; O = a limited physical exam) in order to *reassess* (A) the patient's progress, *plan* (P) any necessary change in nursing actions and implement them. The next progress note repeats the "mini-cycle":

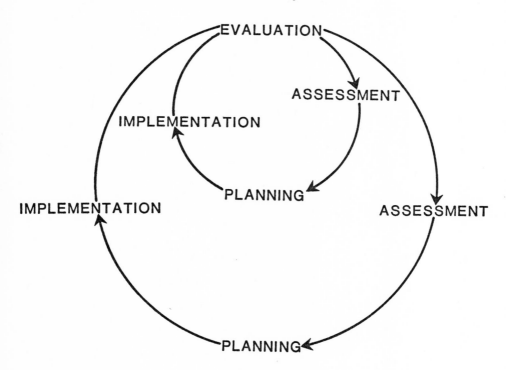

The "mini-cycle" can be thought of as evaluation of progress in reaching an objective, and the larger cycle of the nursing process as evaluation of progress in reaching a goal. Therefore, in carrying out a nursing care plan designed to reach a therapeutic goal (an immediate outcome), many evaluations will be made (progress notes written) of the effectiveness of the nursing actions designed to meet the objectives (intermediate outcomes) necessary to reach the therapeutic goal. Since the nursing actions may be changed, and new objectives may be identified each time progress notes are written, the nursing care plan is constantly being updated or reaffirmed. This is what is meant by a dynamic nursing care plan.

Chapter 14

Patient Care Conferences

In chapter 13 we described the process of day-to-day evaluation of the patient's progress toward attaining the therapeutic objectives in the written nursing care plan. This evaluation was documented as problem-oriented progress notes. The evaluation addressed each of the patient's problems separately and related to therapeutic *objectives* (intermediate outcomes).

In this chapter, we will describe the evaluation that is conducted at patient care conferences. This evaluation looks at progress made for all the patient's problems at a point in time, because the evaluation is related to therapeutic goals (immediate outcomes) requiring a specific level of care. The expectations for this evaluation mechanism are multiple:

1. An overview evaluation of the patient's status

2. Assessment of the need for a specific level of care (utilization review)

3. Discharge planning

4. Retrospective quality of care audit

5. Continuing (inservice) education

To meet these expectations, patient care conferences should include the entire patient care team. All nursing personnel should be involved—nursing administrator, nursing supervisor, restorative nurses, charge nurses, staff nurses, LPNs, and nursing attendants. Other allied health professionals should also be involved—physical therapists, occupational therapists, social service workers, dietitians, etc. The medical director and the patient's physician should also be involved.

The frequency and length of patient care conferences will vary with the way they are organized or structured. For example, a monthly patient care conference may be held only for the purpose of retrospective quality of care audit. Since it is essential for physicians (including those designated by the local PSRO) to attend retrospective audit meetings (see chapter 8), a regularly scheduled monthly conference lasting 45 to 60 minutes is more likely to assure physician attendance.

Inservice educational conferences may also be scheduled periodically. The need for these educational programs is identified through both the concurrent and retrospective audits. The program should never exceed one hour.

It is suggested that routine patient care conferences be scheduled daily at shift changes. This permits two teams involved in the patient care to participate. If one case is scheduled each day, the conference need not exceed 15 minutes. This permits each patient to be evaluated at least once every six weeks (assuming there are less than 45 patients on a nursing unit). The assessment of the need for a specific level of care is of vital importance for utilization review purposes. The evaluation of a patient scheduled for utilization review should be performed a day or two before the utilization review committee is scheduled to meet.

An overview of the patient's status is accomplished by evaluating each of the patient's problems. Several questions should be asked about each problem. Is timely progress being made in reaching the therapeutic goal? Is the time frame for reaching the goal still realistic? Has each of the intermediate outcomes been realized in the time frame expected? If not, is a change in the length of time for reaching the goal required? Are the nursing actions written for each objective adequate? Are other nursing actions required? When should this problem be evaluated again? Does the patient still require a skilled or intermediate level of care for this problem? The answers to some of these questions can be found in the problem-oriented progress notes. The answers to others require the input of varied members of the health care team.

Again, we see that the team is participating in a mini-cycle of the nursing process related to each problem in this evaluation. The summation of the evaluation for all problems results in an understanding of the patient's status. The need for a specific level of care is identified. Also, a realistic identification of the potential disposition of the patient is possible; this should result in a specific discharge plan based on a realistic time frame. These results of the patient care conference evaluation should also be documented in the progress notes by the charge nurse.

Chapter 15

Patient Classification for Long Term Care

Although not an essential part of the quality assurance program, a patient classification system is a useful tool that can be used for the following purposes:

1. Statistical and epidemiological reporting

2. Determination of the appropriate *level* of care (skilled, intermediate, custodial) for:

    A. Financial billing

    B. Third party reimbursement

    C. Utilization Review Committee

    D. PSRO requirements (Medicare and Medicaid)

These data collected and documented during the nursing assessment, planning, and implementation process can be utilized to complete the patient classification. As you performed the nursing history and physical and documented your findings on the appropriate forms, you noted certain elements were weighted by numbers appearing in ☐ . Not all elements were weighted. Weights were assigned only to those elements which are known to affect the intensity of nursing care required by a patient. The magnitude of the weight assigned was determined by reference to a similar classification system developed at Greenbriar Terrace Healthcare, Nashua, New Hampshire by William Thoms, regional director, First Healthcare Corporation. (See Appendix C.) The weights assigned in the Greenbriar system represent minutes of nursing time required to perform specific tasks and procedures; the sums of total units, therefore, represent the minutes of nursing personnel time that must be devoted to a specific patient on a daily basis. Similarly, the total points representing the sum of all weighted units in this classification system should approximate the total minutes of nursing personnel time required daily to provide nursing care for a specific patient. Likewise, the sum of points rated on all patients should equal the total minutes of nursing care required for the nursing units and the entire nursing home. These data, therefore, become a basic tool for the director of nursing service to assign patients to a specific unit to balance the home's nursing load among the various nursing units or to increase staffing on units with a heavy load.

This classification system is also designed to identify care requiring the knowledge and skills of an RN and that which can be performed by nonskilled nursing personnel. In the classification summary, weighted units using guidelines 1, 2, and 3 for nursing actions identify skilled nursing minutes. All other units identify nonskilled nursing minutes.

This classification system also has the potential for use as a guide for reimbursement for the nursing component of long term care. Total minutes of nursing care required for a patient (skilled plus nonskilled) multiplied by the cost per minute of nursing care equals total nursing care costs. Charges for each patient can then be based on actual costs rather than a per diem rate for each level of care. Since in many instances cost of providing high quality care for patients classified as intermediate or custodial is greater than for some classified as skilled, this system could lead to a more equitable and realistic reimbursement mechanism.

Examples of its completion and use are demonstrated in the case presentation provided in Appendix B. Mrs. W. T. is an actual patient cared for at the Near North Pavilion, Illinois Masonic Medical Center. According to the weighted units in the Patient Care Plan, Mrs. W. T.'s nursing care requirements totaled 314 points. This means that Mrs. W. T. would require 314 minutes (or 5 hours and 14 minutes) of total nursing care per day. Of this 314 minutes, 44 were attributable to nursing actions requiring the skills of an RN (that is, used nursing guidelines 1, 2, or 3 in classifying the nursing actions that were written). This classification, therefore, can be utilized by the charge nurse to estimate the staffing requirements to provide Mrs. W. T. with quality care on a daily basis. Similarly, if all other patients on her unit were classified, this system would enable her to plan more appropriately for the staffing of her entire unit.

The reader is also referred to Appendix C, which provides for other classification systems in use in long term care. The classification system originated by William Thoms in New Hampshire was also utilized for classifying Mrs. W. T. In the Thoms classification system, Mrs. W. T. requires 315 minutes of total nursing care time per day, which is nearly identical with the results obtained through the classification system used in this text.

These classification systems have great significance in improving the reimbursement mechanism for long term care. Costs of nursing care can now be separated from the basic per diem "room and board" rates. Minutes of nursing time required for quality care can be multiplied by the hourly cost of nursing personnel to establish the actual cost of nursing care for each patient. This could lead to much more equitable reimbursement policies than those currently employed which establish per diem rates for arbitrary levels of care. Several states, notably West Virginia and Tennessee, are currently experimenting with such reimbursement mechanisms.

NEAR NORTH PAVILION, ILLINOIS MASONIC MEDICAL CENTER
PATIENT CLASSIFICATION

Based on following component of patient assessment:

1. Physician's Care Plan

    A. Medical status: Risk Factor Measurements

        1. Compare height and weight with standard tables (M/F)
           Rate 1 unit for each 10 lbs. overweight

           COMPUTATION:

           Ht. _____ Wt. _____ lbs. overweight $\dfrac{}{10}$ =   ☐

           ┌──┐
           │ EXAMPLE: Ht. 6'0" Wt. 219 Lbs. overweight $\dfrac{39}{10}$ = $\boxed{4}$ │
           └──┘

        2. Blood pressure
           Rate 1 unit for each 20 mm Hg. over 130 systolic
           Rate 1 unit for each 10 mm Hg. over 80 diastolic

           COMPUTATION:

           Systolic BP _____ mm Hg − 130 = $\dfrac{}{20}$ =   ☐

           Diastolic BP _____ mm Hg − 80 = $\dfrac{}{10}$ =   ☐

           ┌──┐
           │ EXAMPLE: │
           │ Systolic BP 156 mm Hg − 130 = $\dfrac{26}{20}$ = $\boxed{1}$ │
           │   │
           │ Diastolic BP 100 mm Hg − 80 = $\dfrac{20}{10}$ = $\boxed{2}$ │
           └──┘

        3. Blood cholesterol (mg %) _____   ☐
              Rate 1 unit if over 300 mg%
              Rate "0" if under 300 mg%

        4. Albuminuria (0 to 4 +)
           Rate 1 unit for every 2 + result

           COMPUTATION:

           Albuminuria $\dfrac{}{2}$ ☐

           ┌──┐
           │ EXAMPLES: │
           │ $\dfrac{1+}{2} = 0;$ $\dfrac{3+}{2} = 1$ │
           └──┘

NEAR NORTH PAVILION, ILLINOIS MASONIC MEDICAL CENTER
PATIENT CLASSIFICATION (Continued)

    5. Cigarette Smoking
       Present smoker (cigarettes/day) _____ /day
       Rate 1 unit for each *pack* of cigarettes smoked/day.
       COMPUTATION:

       Cigarettes smoked/day _____
                               20   = ☐

       ┌───┐
       │ EXAMPLE: │
       │   Cigarettes smoked/day $\frac{50}{20}$ = ②   │
       │   │
       └───┘

1. Physician's Care Plan
   A. Risk Factors

                                      Sub-total units   ☐ 1.A.

   B. Medically Defined Conditions

       Rate 1 unit of *each* of the currently present
       diseases specified in list.   Sub-total units   ☐ 1.B.

2. Nursing History and Physical

   A. Functioning status

       1. Mobility level
          Classify patient as basically
          Bed patient _____
          Chair patient _____
          Ambulatory _____
          Assign appropriate units on functional status summary sheet on reverse of this
          page.

       2. Others
          Refer to Nursing History, "Functional Status" evaluation. For each functional
          (transferring, walking, wheeling, etc.) level checked which has an assigned
          weight unit   ┌─────┐
                        │ No. │
                        └─────┘

          place appropriate units in boxes   ☐   on Functional

       Status Summary sheet on reverse of this page.

   B. Impairments

       Rate 1 unit for each impairment identified *for which the patient has not compen-
       sated* to "normal" function.

                               TOTAL UNITS   ☐ 2.B.

FUNCTIONAL STATUS SUMMARY

FUNCTIONARY STATUS	BED PATIENT	CHAIR	AMBULATORY	PATIENT RATING UNITS
Mobility Level	[36]	[8]	[0]	☐
Transferring	NA	[0] , [4] or [16]	[0] or [4]	☐
Walking	NA		[0] or [16]	☐
Wheeling	NA	[0] , [4] or [8]	[0] , [4] or [8]	☐
Stair Climbing	NA		[0] or [8]	☐
Bathing	[20]	[0] , [18] or [20]	[0] or [18]	☐
Dressing	NA	[0] , [5] , [20] or [30]	[0] , [5] , [20] or [30]	☐
Eating/Feeding	[0] , [20] or [45]	[0] , [20] or [45]	[0] , [20] or [45]	☐
Toileting	[0]* or [8] **	[0] or [8]	[0] or [8]	☐
Bowel Function	[0] or [18]	[0] or [18]	[0] or [18]	☐
Bladder Function	[0] , [20] , [48] or [50]	[0] or [20] , [48] or [50]	[0] or [20] , [48] or [50]	☐
Orientation	[0] , [8] , [16] or [36]	[0] or [8] or [16]	[0] or [8] or [16]	☐
Communication of Needs	[0] , [4] or [8]	[0] , [4] or [8]	[0] , [4] or [8]	☐
Behavior	[0] to [24]	[0] to [24]	[0] to [24]	☐
TOTAL UNITS				☐

2.A.

*Bed patient with bowel and/or bladder dysfunction (see next two items).
**Bed patient using bed pan/urinal with no bowel or bladder dysfunction.

NEAR NORTH PAVILION, ILLINOIS MASONIC MEDICAL CENTER
PATIENT CLASSIFICATION (Continued)

Based on following component of patient assessment:

3. Nursing Actions

A. For *each problem* identified, rate units according to goals (imediate outcome) and restorative potential.

> 5 units for each problem in which the goal is restoration to maximum potential.
>
> 1 unit for each problem in which the goal is only maintenance.

In this classification system, nursing actions are not weighted for more than 6 problems. Therefore, the patient's 6 most important problems should be selected for this classification of nursing actions. Use the *same* problems for rating nursing actions under parts A and B. (Refer to Classification Summary sheet, page 130.)

☐ 3.A.

B. For *each problem*, rate *specific* nursing actions ordered for *any objective* (intermediate outcome) according to the following guidelines. For each of the seven guidelines that follow, consider all specific nursing actions to determine which guideline applies, 1 through 7; rate only *once* for each *problem* in rank order; rate for guideline 1, if applicable, before using guideline 2; guideline 2 before guideline 3; etc.

Guideline 1. Nursing action requiring *procedure* to be *performed* by an RN (skilled nursing procedure). (Includes RN evaluation.)

15 units if performed daily	X _____* =
5 units if performed 3 times a week	X _____* =
3 units if performed less than 3 times a week	X _____* = _____
	Sum

☐ 3.B.1

Guideline 2. Nursing action requiring *judgment* of an RN (skilled nursing supervision) as to where and if a PRN medication (other than laxatives, HS sedation, nonprescription meds) is given, a procedure performed, or patient observed for development of a specific potential problem that appears on the problem list. (Includes RN evaluation.)

15 units if required daily	X _____* =
5 units if required 3 times a week	X _____* =
3 units if required less than 3 times a week	X _____* = _____
	Sum

☐ 3.B.2.

*Total problems for which guideline applies.

NEAR NORTH PAVILION, ILLINOIS MASONIC MEDICAL CENTER
PATIENT CLASSIFICATION (Continued)

Based on following component of patient assessment:

Guideline 3. Nursing action requiring *evaluation* by an RN (skilled nursing supervision/evaluation)

10 units if required daily   X _____* =

5 units if required 3 times a week   X _____* =

3 units if required less than 3 times a week   X _____* = _____

                                   Sum

                                ☐ 3.B.3.

Nursing action requiring a procedure to be performed by nursing personnel other than an RN (non-skilled nursing procedure). Do not include any non-skilled nursing actions that would duplicate rating for care provided for functional disabilities (previously rated on page 126).

NOTE: 1, 2, and 3 above also apply to skilled professional services provided by a *physical therapist, speech therapist* and/or *clinical psychologist.*

Guideline 4. Nursing action (non-skilled) requiring standard nursing procedures (see procedure book) (such as routine back care).

3 units if performed daily   X _____* =

1 unit if performed 3 times a week   X _____* = _____

                                   Sum

                                ☐ 3.B.4.

Guideline 5. Nursing action (non-skilled) requiring a variation from standard or routine nursing procedures (see procedure book) (such as crush all medications, special back care, etc.).

5 units if required daily   X _____* =

2 units if required 3 times a week   X _____* =

1 unit if required less than 3 times a week   X _____* = _____

                                   Sum

                                   3.B.5.

Guideline 6. Nursing action requiring orientation therapy

3 units   X _____ =   ☐ 3.B.6

Guideline 7. Other attitudinal therapy.

3 units   X _____ =   ☐ 3.B.7

                               TOTAL
                               ALL PROBLEMS   ☐

*Total problems for which guide applies.

NEAR NORTH PAVILION, ILLINOIS MASONIC MEDICAL CENTER
PATIENT CLASSIFICATION (Continued)

4. Evaluation of appropriate level of care

☐ Skilled nursing level. This level is justified if:

   1. An RN is required to *perform daily* a skilled nursing procedure (nursing action guideline 1).
   2. An RN is required to make skilled nursing *judgments daily* (nursing action guideline 2).
   3. An RN is required to *evaluate daily* non-skilled tasks and procedures performed by others (nursing action guideline 3).
   4. An RN is required to do any one of 1, 2, or 3 (above) every other day *and* another skilled professional is providing rehabilitation services on the alternate days (physical therapist, speech therapist, occupational therapist [*therapeutic only;* not diversional], clinical psychologist, psychiatric social worker).

☐ Intermediate care level. This level is justified if patient is receiving care as identified in No. 1 through No. 4 under skilled nursing, but *not on a daily basis.*

☐ Custodial care. This level is justified if maintenance is only goal and no specific nursing actions are required.

(Check appropriate level on summary sheet.)

5. DNS statement of level of care.
   (Initial Utilization Review certification)
   I believe, based on the foregoing documentation of nursing care needs of
   _____ that he/she requires_____
   (Patient)
   _____ level of care for at least
   (Level specification)
   _____ days. The patient's continued need for this level of care will be reevaluated
   (number)
   by the Utilization Review Committee on _____.
                                                              (date)
   _____ (Date) _____ RN, DNS

Approved by Utilization Committee

                              _____
                              Chairman, UR Committee

                              _____
                              Date

The Utilization Review Committee disagrees with the assessment and declares a
_____ level of care is required. The patient's continued need will be
reevaluated on _____.
                                      (date)
_____ Chairman, UR Committee   _____ Date

_____ Medical Director   _____ Date

_____ Nursing Home Administrator _____ Date

PATIENT CARE CLASSIFICATION SUMMARY   NEAR NORTH PAVILION, ILLINOIS MASONIC MEDICAL CENTER

Patient _____   Patient Number _____

Data Source	Evaluation Elements	Initial Evaluation Total Units (date)	Subsequent Evaluations Units (date)	Units (date)	Units (date)
Physician's Care Plan	A. Risk Factors				
	B. Current Diseases				
Nursing History and Physicial	A. Functional Status				
	B. Impairments				

Nursing Actions

	# of Problem Rated (See Problem List)	A. Goal/Units (Restorative = 5) (Maintenance = 1) for Problem Rated	B. Specific Actions — Check (x) Guideline Which Applies							Units			
			1	2	3	4	5	6	7				
1.													
2.													
3.													
4.													
5.													
6.													

Use these blocks on subsequent evaluations to note problem numbers of problems *rated*. (See problem list.) Also note total number of *active* problems as of this date.

Total # of Active Problems	Total Units	
	Total Units/Goals	

Level of Care		
Skilled		
Intermediate		
Custodial		

TOTAL POINTS (Add All Evaluation Units)

On this sheet enter totals from appropriate ☐ from evaluation summary

NEAR NORTH PAVILION, ILLINOIS MASONIC MEDICAL CENTER
ANALYSIS OF PATIENT CARE REQUIREMENTS AS OF

_____ (date)

Patient Name	Pat. No.	Room No.	# of Problems	Care Level*	Total Points =	Physician's Care Plan		Nursing History & Physical		Nursing Actions		Remarks
						Risk Factors +	Current Diseases +	Functional Status +	Impairments +	Goal (Restorative Potential) +	Total Units +	

Total Points

* Note Code

S = Skilled

I = Intermediate

C = Custodial

R = Residential

Chapter 16

Discharge Planning

In the past, discharge planning in the health field has usually been limited to the acute, short term hospital setting. The nursing home has frequently been the placement site, resulting from the hospital's discharge planning process. External regulation of the hospital by Medicare and Medicaid and Professional Standards Review Organizations (PSROs) has led to the development of sophisticated hospital discharge planning programs. These same regulations have been extended to long term care facilities.

The discharge planning process is important for the long term care facility. This is particularly true for the skilled nursing home which is oriented toward a restorative nursing program. The purpose of restorative nursing is to enable patients to care for themselves as independently as possible, compatible with their state of health. Some patients will be able to return to total independent living in their own homes; others will require some degree of support services. This could vary from temporary help through a home care program to a permanent placement in a residential or sheltered care environment.

In chapter 2 of this text it was pointed out that a change in environment can produce severe stress in the elderly patient to the degree that such change itself can frequently lead to increased mortality. While this is particularly true when a patient moves from a familiar home environment to a long term care facility, it is equally true when the patient leaves the protective custody of the long term care facility to return to a less protected, more independent environment. The need for planning for this change requires time and active involvement of the patient in the planning process. It is dangerous to the patient's health to think of discharge planning at the point of discharge. Discharge planning should be an ongoing factor in the continuing care of the patient and should be an integral part of the total care plan in which the patient participates.

The patient's family is also a vital element in the planning process. A period of time should be planned in which those responsible for the patient's care after discharge actually have the opportunity to perform new and unfamiliar activities under supervision to insure success. Both the nurse and social workers should visit the patient's home to insure that the new environment is compatible with the patient's functioning abilities. For example, a patient who has had a fractured hip may have difficulty in the toileting function if required to use the commode found in most homes. Raising the seat of the toilet approximately six inches and providing for the installation of hand rails on both sides of the commode may be necessary before the patient is discharged. Potential hazardous conditions in the home should be discussed openly and frankly with the patient's family. For example, scatter rugs on the floor may cause an increased hazard to the patient who requires a cane or a walker.

Social workers are important members of discharge planning teams because of their knowledge of community resources. Access to these resources, such as visiting nurse services or coordinated home care programs, may be necessary to consider in the decision making process for future patient discharge. Community agencies that will be involved in the patient's future care should be encouraged to visit the patient while still institutionalized in the long term care facility to provide for the transition to the new environment.

The reader is referred to Appendix A, which is a model utilization review plan, and particularly to paragraph XIII, Policy on Discharge Planning. Discharge planning is now mandated in most utilization review programs, and Appendix A will provide insight into the appropriate integration of the discharge planning process in the overall utilization review plan. The reader is again cautioned, however, that such external regulations may encourage a patient's discharge on short notice. Such pressures should be anticipated so that the time required for an orderly transfer of the patient to a new environment can be totally planned.

Appendix A

Near North Pavilion—IMMC
Administrative Patient Care Policies

Effective: September 1, 1976

Administrative
Functional
Responsibility: Director of Nursing Service

Clinical Functional
Responsibility: Utilization Review
                          Committee Chairman

UTILIZATION REVIEW PLAN

I. PURPOSE

Utilization Review has as its overall objectives both the maintenance of high quality patient care and assurance of appropriate and efficient utilization of facility services. There are two elements to Utilization Review: Medical Care Evaluation studies that identify and examine patterns of care provided in the facility, and review of extended duration cases which are concerned with efficiency, appropriateness and cost effectiveness of care.

II. OBJECTIVE

To assure that this facility has explored all possible options and utilized those procedures which demonstrate the fullest possible consideration of the patient's health care needs and restorative potential.

III. PROCESS

An ongoing review will be conducted by the Utilization Review Committee which devotes its attention to whether the procedure was necessary, whether the best possible alternative was selected to meet the patient's needs, and to assess the quality of the services that were provided.

IV. STRUCTURE OF COMMITTEE

The utilization review function is conducted by a staff committee composed of two or more physicians, with participation of other professional personnel, or by a group outside the facility which is similarly composed. Review by the committee may not be conducted by any person who is employed by or who is financially interested in any skilled nursing facility or by any person who was professionally involved in the care of a patient whose case is being reviewed.

Wherever a local Professional Standards Review Organization (PSRO) is operative, this delegated Utilization Review Committee will then seek its approval. The prime responsibility for the direction of committee activities will belong to the selected physician chairman.

All reviews will have medical direction and medical determinations made, particularly concerning a medical determination to deny benefits.

Other professional personnel may participate on the Utilization Review Committee, however, all determinations are made exclusively by the physician members of the committee.

V. FUNCTIONING OF UTILIZATION REVIEW COMMITTEE

The physician members will follow the current Medicare Guidelines as stipulated in Section 200 of the Skilled Nursing Facility Manual. Patient length of stay parameters will be based on the statistical accumulation of data compiled by the Fiscal Intermediary.

The Committee may also develop and follow its own length of stay parameters, based on the statistical accumulation of IMMC data as it relates to current experience.

The Committee may approve or deny (after proper consultation with the attending physician) based on the certification or recertification, and the plan of treatment established by the attending physician. The admission certification and first recertification must be done by the attending physician or a physician on the staff of the facility who has knowledge of the case.

The second and subsequent recertifications may be completed by the physician members of the Utilization Review Committee. The Committee may have access to all pertinent medical, nursing and rehabilitation documentation, which is to be found in medical records as specified in the Concurrent Review Section of the Quality Assurance Program.

Designated personnel of the Skilled Nursing Facility will be responsible for notifying the attending physician and the patient or his representative in writing within two (2) days of a determination to deny Medicare benefits.

VI.   EXTENDED DURATION REVIEW

Primarily two (2) types of review will be accomplished:

A.   *Continuing Patient Assessment*

The term "Extended Duration Review" will be hereafter referred to as "Continuing Patient Assessment."

"Continuing Patient Assessment" is a form of length of stay review which evaluates the patient's needs of in-patient skilled nursing and rehabilitative services, thus assuring that the services are medically necessary, reasonable and appropriate.

The review is based on the attending physician's reasons for and plan for continued stay and any other documentation the Committee or group deems appropriate. Cases may be screened by a qualified nonphysician representative of the Committee or group who uses criteria established by the physician members of the Committee, provided that cases are referred to a physician member for further review when it appears that the patient no longer requires in-patient care. Where the Committee or group selects a nonphysician representative to screen extended stay review cases, it will select an individual with experience in such screening or appropriate training in the application of the screening criteria used, or both.

Based on the initial nursing care plan and nursing care evaluation, the Director of Nursing Service will assign an appropriate number of continuous days of coverage for each patient. The number of days assigned can be based on sources of norms for problem-specific length of stay (LOS) in Skilled Nursing Facilities. (In no case can an initial length of stay be assigned for more than thirty (30) days and subsequent length of stay for longer than thirty (30) day intervals. See below concerning patient re-certification.)

The Utilization Review Committee may confirm the initial length of stay, assigned by the Director of Nursing Service, between the third and seventh day after admission. (In those areas where community-based Skilled Nursing Facility review is carried out by physician organizations, state Medicaid agencies, or Professional Standards Review Organizations, this confirmation can be obtained from the review organization or their Utilization Review Coordinator by telephone.)

The Utilization Review Committee should also reevaluate each patient three days *before* the expiration of the initial length of stay assigned to determine the need for continued stay, recertify, and assign a new review case.

Patient Recertification

The Utilization Review Committee must reevaluate all Title XVIII and Title XIX patients on or before the thirtieth day of care and every thirty (30) days thereafter for their first ninety (90) days of care; then, every ninety (90) days.

To aid the Committee in their reevaluations, the Director of Nursing Service must schedule a patient for nursing care reevaluation at the daily patient care conference, twenty-four (24) hours *before* the Committee reviews the patient.

B. *Medical Care Evaluation Studies*

These studies identify and examine the levels of care required by a patient and the services provided in the Skilled Nursing Facility to fulfill these skilled nursing or rehabilitation requirements, as specified in the Retrospective Review Section of the Quality Assurance Program.

Consistent with the Regulations, Section 405:1137(c), these studies promote the most effective and efficient use of available health facilities and services consistent with patient needs and professionally recognized standards of health care. Studies emphasize identification and analysis of patterns of patient care, and suggest where appropriate, possible changes for maintaining consistently high quality patient care and effective and efficient use of services. Each medical care evaluation study (whether medical or administrative in emphasis) identifies and analyzes factors related to the patient care rendered in the facility, and, where indicated, results in recommendations for change beneficial to patients, staff, the facility and the community. Studies on a sample or other basis include, but need not be limited to: admissions, durations of stay, ancillary services furnished (including drugs and biologicals), and professional services performed on facility premises. At least one study must be in progress at any given time, and at least one study must be completed each year. The results of each study in promoting appropriate use of the facility and improving the quality of care are to be documented.

VII. QUALITY ASSURANCE PROGRAM—MEDICAL CARE EVALUATION STUDIES

This Utilization Review Committee Plan is incorporated within our Quality Assurance Program. The Quality Assurance Program is intended to meet the requirements of Title XVIII and Title XIX review which includes Continuing Patient Assessment and Medical Care Evaluation Studies.

Quality Assurance Program will include three (3) specific programs: Comprehensive Pre-admission Assessment, Continuing Patient Evaluation, and Retrospective Review Program for review as suggested in the Professional Standards Review Organization's manual for Long Term Care Facilities.

A. *Comprehensive Pre-Admission Assessment*

1. The nursing facility will insist that a physician-pre-

pared patient care plan for each patient be documented at the time of admission or as soon as possible within the first forty-eight (48) hours of admission. Patients should not be accepted in transfer unless this documentation precedes or accompanies the patient to the facility.

2. The Director of Nursing Service is responsible for the completion of a comprehensive patient care assessment at the time of admission or as soon as possible within the first forty-eight (48) hours of admission. Such assessment should follow the medical care plan for the patient and result in a specific nursing care plan for each individual patient. The Director of Nursing Service may delegate this task, but must retain the responsibility and function of assigning the initial length of stay for Utilization Review purposes.

3. The patient care plan is to be written and is to be problem oriented.

a. Each of the patient's problems is to be identified and numbered.

b. Goals should be developed for solving each problem based on the patient's restorative potential. A time estimate is to be made for achieving each goal, considering the length of stay guidelines.

c. Specific nursing interventions for each problem are to be identified. This will include specific tasks and procedures performed by various members of the facility health care team in assisting patients to achieve their goals.

B. *Continuing Patient Evaluation*

1. Concurrent Review Program

a. A periodic evaluation of the patient's progress will be documented. The method of documentation will be the patient's progress notes and will be used by all professional members of the facility health care team. This will be the responsibility of the charge nurse in each unit. Frequency of such documentation will depend upon the intensity of illness or care for the patient's specific problems. All documentation should refer to the numbered problems listed on the nursing orders plan. (A problem list should appear as a separate sheet preceding all progress notes.)

Each progress note will contain the following elements of information:

(1) **S** — Subjective complaints and/or comments by the patient related to the problem.

(2) **O** — Observed reactions to the treatment process, as evaluated by the nurse.

(3) **A** — Assessment of the patient's new status at this point in time in relation to the original goal.

(4) **P** — Plan for continued treatment. A specific notation should be made of a change or a continuation of the nursing order plan for this particular problem.

NOTE: It is intended that the first letters of each of these progress charting guidelines spell out the acronym *SOAP*. This acronym will remind the person making the documentation of the necessity of addressing each of these items, in each progress report.

b. In addition to the periodic evaluation of the patient's progress by the charge nurse (see A. of this section), the patient's total care will be periodically evaluated by the entire patient care team: Director of Nursing Service, Charge Nurse, and Nurses' Aides. These conferences should also be attended by other specialists and those other allied health professionals directly involved in the care of the patient, such as the social worker, physical therapists, etc. In this way, each patient's care will be evaluated in an inservice type educational format at least once every ninety (90) days. An estimate must also be made as to this patient's need for continuing care. Patient Care Conferences are basically nursing care conferences, but the facility's medical director and the patient's attending physician should be encouraged to attend. Such Patient Care Conferences should also result in a statement of the nursing staff's estimate as to the patient's continued need for a specific level of care; that is, skilled, intermediate, or residential. A discharge plan must be written as early as possible within the first seven (7) days of admission. Such estimation will be of great value to the Utilization Review Committee in carrying out its function. (See "Continuing Patient Assessment," Section VI, A.)

(1) Discharge Planning (See Section XIII.)

C. *Retrospective Review Program*

The retrospective review program is complementary to the concurrent review program. The concurrent review program has its primary emphasis on *nursing* care evaluation. The restrospective review emphasizes total *patient* care evaluation. The review team must include physicians as well as nurses and administrators.

Conduct of this program will be the primary responsibility of the facility medical director. The program is designed to review the quality of care of all patients admitted to the facility. It is also designed to satisfy the opportunity available under Section 1155(e) of the Professional Standards Review Organization Amendments to PL 92-603; that is, to permit the facility to qualify for a *delegated review function* by the local Professional Standards Review Organization for its Title XVIII and Title XIX patients. Achieving such a qualification will require the addition of physicians, approved by the local Professional Standards Review Organization, to serve on the retrospective review team. The methodology will be adapted as follows by the review team:

1. Develop outcome criteria (goals or objectives) for the status of the patients at the termination of both the skilled and intermediate levels of care for those specific diseases or problems frequently cared for in the nursing facility.

2. A pattern display of actual practice will be provided to the review team. Pattern displays will be developed by medical record personnel from data abstracted from the

medical records of all patients treated over a specific time period for each disease or problem, for which criteria have been developed.

3. The review team will evaluate actual practice as compared with the criteria to identify problem areas needing further study or correction.

The evaluation process will determine whether suboptimal care results from:

a. Performance or attitude of personnel or,

b. Structural organization of care.

If suboptimal care results from either a. or b., inservice education programs or organizational changes will be initiated by the Director of Nursing Service and in consultation with the Nursing Home Administrator.

Such evaluation may require a significant in-depth process audit to determine the reason for suboptimal nursing care. The Phaneuf, Qualpac, or Slater Scale Test may be recommended to the nursing staff by the Director of Nursing Service in such instances.

4. Recommendations for appropriate corrective action will be made in writing to the facility Administrator by the Medical Director or Utilization Review Committee Chairman.

5. The review team will periodically follow-up on its recommendation and determine if suggested corrective actions have been appropriate, as revealed by improved outcomes in subsequent reviews. Medical record personnel will abstract each discharged patient's chart for the criteria for specific disease entities and nursing problems as they are developed.

VIII. OTHER TYPES OF REVIEW—OPTIONAL

At the discretion of the Committee members, review for the following may be accomplished:

A. Cases in conflict with Regulatory Agencies.

B. Cases indicating a change in level of care.

C. Cases that are questioned by the facility's Director of Nursing Service requiring medical consultation and intervention, if necessary.

IX. ADMINISTRATIVE RESPONSIBILITIES

The Administrator of the facility will provide:

A. Personnel necessary to assist the Chairman of the Utilization Review Committee in scheduling meetings.

B. Compilation of data originating from the Medical Care Evaluation Studies.

C. Implementation of recommendations made by the Chairman and Committee members.

D. Consultants as deemed necessary by the Committee.

E. Maintenance of records for the Utilization Review Committee.

X. UTILIZATION REVIEW COMMITTEE RECORDS

Minutes of the Utilization Review Committee activities or those of all full Committee meetings or subcommittee meetings will be maintained by the facility.

In the event that a determination to deny benefits is made by at least two (2) physician members of the committee that a patient does not require a particular level of care according to Title XVIII and Title XIX Guidelines, notification will be given to the attending physician. If the attending physician disagrees with the denial determination and the Committee reaffirms the denial determination, the Administrator will prepare *written* notification to the attending physician, to the patient or his representative, and to the appropriate insurance carrier within forty-eight (48) hours.

If a patient wishes to remain as a private paying patient after his illness has stabilized, such decisions shall be reviewed by the Administrator, the Director of Nursing Service and the Attending Physician. The patient may remain only on their recommendation. Records of such status change need not be processed by the Utilization Review Committee.

The minutes of the Utilization Review Committee meeting will contain the following:

A. Name of Committee

B. Date and place of meeting

C. Times the meeting convened and adjourned

D. Names of Committee members present and absent

E. Review of minutes of previous meeting (optional)

F. Continuing Patient Assessment

1. Patient identification other than name

2. Date of admission

3. Diagnosis

4. Decision reached, rationale for decision reached, date of next review.

G. Medical Care Evaluation Studies

1. Report on the status of each study currently in progress.

2. Summarize study with recommendations and note implementation.

H. Summary

1. *Title XVIII* — This would include the number of extended duration cases reviewed-approved-denied.

   a. Request for concurrence—questionable cases presented and a total number of all cases reviewed.

2. *Title XIX*—Number of cases reviewed-approved for present level of care-denied for lower level of care.

I. Adjournment

The adjournment time and signature of the Chairman of the Committee should be obtained. The signature does not have to be obtained at the time of adjournment. It can be done at the subsequent Utilization Review Committee meeting.

XI. MODEL AGENDA FOR UTILIZATION REVIEW MEETING

This agenda is to be followed during a Utilization Review Committee meeting:

A. Call to Order

B. Roll

    1. Members present

    2. Members absent

C. Reading of Minutes of Previous Meeting

D. Old Business

    1. Follow-up on last month's business, if any

E. New Business

    1. Any new business presented before the Committee

      a. Any discussion in which the members of the Committee contributed

    2. Report from Subcommittee meetings—either separate minutes or included in full Committee minutes

    3. Reviews

      a. Extended Duration Reviews—for Medicare, patient must be reviewed within (thirty (30) days and thirty (30) days thereafter. For all other patients, reviews shall be accomplished every thirty-sixty-ninety (30-60-90) days based on medical and nursing necessity to be determined by the Utilization Review Committee.

      b. Cases in conflict—See Section VIII, "Other Types of Review."

      c. Admissions—questionable for medical necessity or admission of cases denied by Director of Nursing Services and requires Utilization Review Committee concurrence.

      d. Medical Care Evaluation Study—(If none presented, state, "in process.")

        (1) Title of study

(2) Definition (purpose) of study

(3) Number of patients studied and/or

(4) Worksheets of study

(5) Findings of study

(6) Conclusions (by Committee)

(7) Recommendations (by Committee)

(8) Follow-up (by Committee, if none, state, "none.")

F. Summary of Utilization Review Committee Determinations:

1. Medicare Reviewed (Title XVIII)

   a. approved
   b. denied

2. Medicaid Reviewed (Title XIX)

   a. approved for present level of care
   b. denied—lower level of care

3. Other:

G. Adjournment

H. Signature of Chairman

1. Not to be signed until presented to full Committee for approval.

XII. UTILIZATION REVIEW FLOW SHEET — *(Exhibit 1, Following)*

A. *Introduction*

The flow sheet that follows is a diagram that will assist administration and professional members of the Utilization Review Committee to perform the steps necessary for effective functioning of Utilization Review. This flow sheet follows the line of communication necessary for the effective functioning of any Utilization Review Committee and outlines the instruction contained in Section 405:1137, *Conditions of Participation* for Skilled Nursing Facilities. It is intended to be used as a tool for

Exhibit 1

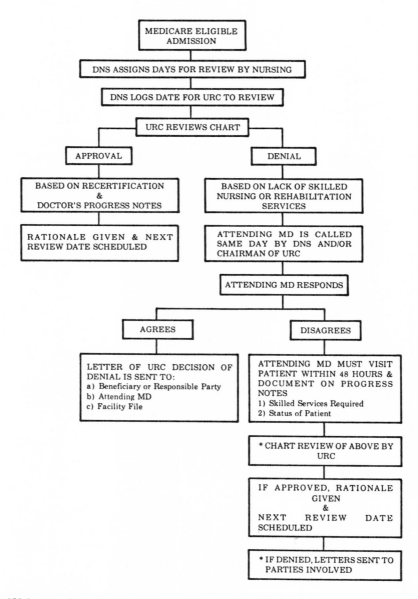

*If the attending physician feels case is covered and the Utilization Review Committee disagrees, this is an opportunity for peer consultation.

Two Committee physicians' signatures are required to deny Medicare benefits.

proper review of clinical records, proper review of medical procedures, proper and correct notification to the attending physician and the patient in the event of a denial.

Please note, in the event of a denial, this is an opportunity for the attending physician to be contacted by a fellow physician and a discussion to follow regarding the necessity of medical documentation and thus increase the attending physician's understanding of Title XVIII and Title XIX, Regulations and Guidelines.

XIII. POLICY ON DISCHARGE PLANNING

A. *Introduction*

This facility is to have a centralized coordinated discharge planning program which ensures that each patient's need for a planned program of expected duration will include his or her post-discharge needs.

The Utilization Review Committee, in its evaluation of the correct status of each extended duration case should be informed of the results of such discharge planning by the Director of Nursing Service, who is the person designated by the Administrator to be in charge of discharge planning and coordination of services. Information on alternatives available through community resources to which the patient may be referred, will be given by the Director of Nursing Service at the monthly Utilization Review Committee meeting.

B. *Discharge Planning Procedure*

1. Director of Nursing Service*

a. Function—will review each case within seven (7) days following admission to the facility and in consultation with the Administrator, the patient's family, the patient's physician, and the patient, and will develop an appropriate discharge plan. This initial discharge plan will then be periodically updated.

b. Authority—The Director of Nursing Service acts in a singular capacity as coordinator.

---

*Note: These functions may be delegated by the DNS to the Social Service Director.

2. Time Periods in Planning

a. All patients shall be reviewed and a discharge plan determined preferably at admission, but not later than seven (7) days thereafter.

b. Each patient's discharge plan will be updated periodically as needed with a reevaluation made at least every ninety (90) days.

3. Resources

a. Home Health Services, Community Nursing Services, and Homemaker Services will be used by the Director of Nursing Service as the general informational source as to availability of services.

b. A list of these local resources will be in the facility; i.e., Home Health Agencies, Board and Care Facilities, Family Counseling Services, Intermediate Care Facilities.

c. Contact will be made with the Public Health Nurse of the community where the facility is located for assistance in becoming more familiar with services which may be utilized in discharge planning and home care.

4. Review of Discharge Planning Program

a. The Discharge Planning Program will have an Advisory Committee consisting of the Administrator, the Medical Director or Attending Physician, and other appropriate consultants as indicated who will meet annually to evaluate the effectiveness of the program. The other appropriate consultants will include but not be limited to the Dietitian, Pharmacist, Therapist, Activity Director, Social Worker, and Facility Staff (both licensed and non-licensed).

b. The Director of Nursing Service will report quarterly to the Administrator and make recommendations concerning how the program might be improved.

5. Records

a. The current discharge plan for each patient will be a permanent part of the patient's medical record.

b. A Pre-Discharge Appraisal of Home Care Needs form is to be used by the facility and will include the following:
(1) Patient's name
(2) Current physician's orders
(3) Medications
(4) Diet
(5) Current physical and mental status of patient
(6) Special equipment required
(7) Additional comments
(See Exhibit 2 immediately following.)

c. The form, "Family Guide for Care of the Patient at Home," will be used by the facility to aid the family in caring for the discharged patient at home. (See Exhibit 3 immediately following.) This form is to accompany the patient at the time of discharge and is to be discussed with the family prior to discharge. The form will contain the following information:
(1) Patient's name
(2) Next appointment with physician, if known
(3) Current medication and diet
(4) Current physical and mental status of patient
(5) Other nursing needs
(6) Community agency contact

d. The "Patient Care Referral Form" (two pages) will be completed prior to discharge of a patient who will require services of Community Nursing Services. The original will be sent to the receiving agency through the mail after the Charge Nurse has made contact with the agency and communicated patient diagnosis, physician orders, medications and nursing care plan.
(See Exhibit 4 immediately following.)

Exhibit 2

NEAR NORTH PAVILION, ILLINOIS MASONIC MEDICAL CENTER

PRE-DISCHARGE APPRAISAL OF HOME CARE NEEDS

Patient's Name _____

A. Summary of Patient's Salient Dysfunctions (e.g. mental condition; mobility status; continence; communications; sensory perception; etc.):

_____

_____

_____

_____

B. Summary of Nursing Needs:

Help in feeding _____	Nutritional teaching _____	Ambulation _____
Help with bathing _____	Full bed bath _____	Help in dressing _____
Bedpan and/or urinal _____	Skin care _____	Help in hair care _____
Injections _____	Supervision/teaching or	Help in shaving _____
Medications (oral) _____	self-injection _____	Irrigations _____
Help in transfers _____	Dressings _____	Exercise _____
Other:		

_____

_____

C. Other Treatment Needs (e.g., physical therapy, etc.): _____

_____

_____

D. Special Equipment/Supplies Needed: _____

_____

_____

E. Additional Comments: _____

_____

_____

_____

Appraisal by (title, signature) _____

_____
Date

Exhibit 3

NEAR NORTH PAVILION, IMMC

FAMILY GUIDE FOR CARE OF THE PATIENT AT HOME

Patient's Name: _____

Next appointment with physician: _____ Date: _____ Time: _____

Current Medications: (Include name, amount and time of day to be given.)

_____

_____

_____

Diet: _____

Current physical and mental status of patient:

Ambulation	Independent	Needs Assistance	Unable	Comments
Bed-to-chair				
Walking				
Stairs				
Wheelchair				
Crutches				
Cane				
Bed Rest				

Activities				
Bathes self				
Dresses self				
Feeds self				
Brushes teeth				
Shaves self				
Toilet				
Commode				
Bed pan				
Urinal				

Communication Comments:

( ) Verbal _____
( ) Non-verbal _____

Exhibit 3 (Continued)

FAMILY GUIDE FOR CARE OF THE PATIENT AT HOME

Behaviour Comments:

( ) Alert _____
( ) Forgetful _____
( ) Noisy _____
( ) Withdrawn _____
( ) Confused _____
( ) Other _____

Other nursing needs:

Exercise Program, i.e., range of motion _____
Dressing changes _____
Administration of Medications (state if patient requires assistance, and what kind)_____

_____

_____

Administration of Injections _____
Irrigations _____ Catheter _____ Stomas _____

_____

_____

Community Agency Contact: (i.e. local VNA, Home Health Agency, Family Service, etc.)

Name: _____

Address: _____

Telephone Number _____

_____
Signature

Exhibit 4

NEAR NORTH PAVILION, ILLINOIS MASONIC MEDICAL CENTER

PATIENT CARE REFERRAL FORM

Patient's Facility Record # _____

PATIENT

FROM _____ NAME _____

Unit/clinic _____ ADDRESS _____

ADDRESS _____ _____ TEL. _____

_____ TEL. _____ FLOOR ____ APT. ____ BIRTHDATE _____

ADM.   DISC.   AGE   SEX   MARITAL STATUS   RELIGION

DATE   DATE   M F   S M W D SEP

                                                        RELATIVE OR

TO: _____ GUARDIAN _____

ADDRESS _____ ADDRESS _____

_____ TEL. _____ _____ TEL. _____

MEDICARE # & LETTER   PLAN   BLUE CROSS #   SOC. SEC. #   OTHER
                                         A   B

MEDICARE COVERED DAYS   UR REVIEW DATE   APP. ____ DENIAL

_____   FROM: _____ TO: _____

(Exhibit 4 continues on page 156.)

Exhibit 4 (Continued)

PATIENT CARE REFERRAL FORM

DIAGNOSIS(es) Surgery Performed and Date, Allergies or Infections

Is Patient ( ) Family ( ) aware of diagnosis: yes ( ) no ( )   Date of last physical:

PHYSICIAN'S ORDERS: (Include specific orders for Diet, Lab Tests,
                     Speech and O.T.)   Transport By: Ambulance ( ) Car ( )

MEDICATION	STRENGTH & FREQUENCY	DATE & TIME OF LAST DOSE

TREAMENTS & FREQUENCY _____

DIET _____

PHYSICAL THERAPY: Restrict Activity yes ( ) no ( ) Sensation Impaired yes ( ) no ( )
Precautions Weight bearing status — Non-Weight ( ) Partial Weight ( ) Full Weight ( )
SPECIFIC TREATMENT & FREQUENCY _____

ANTICIPATED GOALS _____

REHABILITATION POTENTIAL IS _____

( ) NURSING	OCC ( ) THERAPY	SPEECH ( ) THERAPY	SOCIAL ( ) WORK
HOME HEALTH SERVICES	H.H. ( ) AIDE	PHYSICAL ( ) THERAPY	OTHER ( ) SPECIFY

The above
services require   I   II   III-Inter   IV (Residential)
   Level of Care ( ) Skilled   ( ) Lg. Term   ( ) mediate   ( ) Board & Care
CERTIFICATION (when applicable):
Services above needed to treat condition for which patient
was hospitalized ( ) yes, ( ) no. I certify that the above-   _____ M.D.
named patient is: one.   (Signature)

( ) Under my care (or has been referred to another physi-   _____ M.D.
    cian having professional knowledge of patient's condi-   (Print Name)
    tion), is home bound and requires skilled nursing care
    on an intermittent basis as stated in the orders.   TEL. _____ DATE _____
( ) requires skilled nursing home care on a daily bais for   Will follow ( ) yes, ( ) no -if no, who:
    any of the conditions for which he/she received care
    during SNF stay.   _____ M.D.
( ) requires acute hospital care.

                                    ADDRESS _____ TEL. _____

TO BE COMPLETED BY PHYSICIAN

Exhibit 4 (Continued)

PATIENT CARE REFERRAL FORM

EVALUATION OF PATIENT'S FUNCTIONAL LEVEL	INDE-PEN-DENT	NEEDS ASSIST-ANCE	UN-ABLE	PATIENT CARE PLAN (Explain details of care, medications, treatments, teaching, habits, preferences, diet, and goals.
AMBULATION				
Bed-Chair				
Walking				Medications: Note time last dose
Stairs				given on day of discharge.
Wheelchair				
Crutches				
Walker				
Cane				
ACTIVITIES				
Bathe self				
Dress self				
Feed self				Treatments:
Brushing teeth				
Shaving				
Toilet				
Commode				
Bedpan/urinal				

Bowel & Bladder Program ( ) yes ( ) no
Incontinence: Bladder ( ) Bowel ( )
Date of last enema:
Catheter: Type
Date last changed:
Weight   Height   Date
Anointed   ( ) yes   ( ) no   Special diet instructions:

Check if Pertinent (Describe at right)
DISABILITIES
  ( ) Amputation
  ( ) Paralysis
  ( ) Contractures
  ( ) Decubitus
  ( ) other
IMPAIRMENTS
  ( ) Speech
  ( ) Hearing
  ( ) Vision
  ( ) Sensation
  ( ) Other
COMMUNICATION   Therapies (Pt, OT, Speech):
  ( ) Can write
  ( ) Talks
  ( ) Understands speaking

Exhibit 4 (Continued)

PATIENT CARE REFERRAL FORM

( ) Understands English
( ) If no, other language
( ) Reads
( ) Non-Verbal
BEHAVIOR
( ) Alert
( ) Forgetful
( ) Noisy
( ) Confused
( ) Withdrawn
( ) Wanders
( ) Other
REQUIRES
MARK "S" if self, "N" if needed

( ) Colostomy Care	( ) Dentures
( ) Cane	( ) Eye Glasses
( ) Crutches	( ) Hearing Aid
( ) Walker	( ) Prothesis
( ) Wheelchair	( ) Side Rails
( ) Other	

BRIEF SUMMARY:
(Social Information including patient's personality, attitude toward illness and family, interrelationships, and family's attitude.)

GOALS:

_____
DIRECTOR OF NURSING SERVICE

_____
DATE

Appendix B

Model Patient Care Plan

This model patient care plan is provided for two purposes. First, it permits the reader to visualize the application of the forms provided in the text in the assessment and planning process for a specific patient. Secondly, this appendix can be used as a workbook for self-evaluation of an understanding of the planning portion of the nursing process. It can also be used for this same purpose in inservice education programs.

The case presented, Mrs. W. T., is an actual patient cared for at the Near North Pavilion of the Illinois Masonic Medical Center in Chicago. (The patient's name and certain socio-demographic details have been changed to assure confidentiality.) The discharge summary from the hospital, the physician's care plan, the nursing history and physical exam are provided. After reading these data, the user should develop his own problem list and write nursing actions for each problem. One can also perform the patient classification for Mrs. W. T. Following this exercise, the user can compare his forms with those completed by the nursing staff at the Near North Pavilion.

Discharge Summary, Mrs. W. T.
City Hospital

Mrs. W. T. is an 84 year old white female, admitted to City Hospital on 10/16/76 following an acute stroke. Her past medical history was noncontributory except for known hypertension for 10 years. She had otherwise enjoyed good health. She had never married and since retirement at age 70 has made her home with a younger sister.

The patient was admitted with a complete right hemiplegia. She was comatose. Arteriograms showed severe bilateral carotid arteriosclerosis. Vascular surgical intervention was not considered because of the patient's age, poor condition and the generalized nature of the arteriosclerotic process.

With supportive treatment, her condition gradually improved over a six-week period. She was given physical therapy daily. A gastrostomy was performed two weeks before discharge so that IV feedings could be discontinued. She still has some residual paralysis of the swallowing muscles. A Foley catheter controlled incontinence until it was removed one week before discharge, when bladder training was begun. She has residual weakness of her entire right side.

Patient is to be transferred to a nursing home for restorative nursing care and rehabilitative physical therapy for her residual right hemiplegia.

NEAR NORTH PAVILION, ILLINOIS MASONIC MEDICAL CENTER

REQUEST FOR ADMISSION

On or About ___ 12/1/76 ___

Mrs. W. T.
_____
Patient's Name

City Hospital
_____
Current Place of Residence

If institutionalized, please attach interfacility transfer form and a copy of history, physical examination, and discharge summary.

PHYSICIAN's CARE PLAN

Current Diagnoses	Goals for Restoration/ Rehabilitation	Degree of Restoration Anticipated
Principal		
1. Post CVA; residual rt. hemiplegia ⟶		Anticipate nearly complete recovery.
Secondary		
2. Gastrostomy for feeding ⟶		Use until patient can swallow.
3. Paralysis swallowing muscles ⟶		Anticipate restoration of swallowing function.

Anticipated length of stay in SNF ___ 1-2 months ___

Discharge Plans: Home __X__ with sister   Other Institution _____

Maintenance in SNF _____   Terminal Care _____
ICF_____

Other (specify)_____

Current Treatment Plans: (Outline care to be initiated in the SNF.)

1. Varco gastrostomy feeding 600 cc q 6 hours. Give additional 600 cc water daily.
2. B complex with C (500 mgm.) (pediatric) into gastrostomy feeding.
3. Ambulate with walker → 4 point cane.
4. P.T. consult re right hemiplegic residual.
5. Bowel and bladder training (no catheter!)   *John Doe* M.D.

RISK FACTORS MEASUREMENT (Specify the readings and dates in the spaces provided below.)

	Readings	Date		Readings	Date
Height	5'3"	11/15/76	Blood Choles.	200 mg.	10-20-76
Weight	110	"	BUN	12	"
Blood Pressure	160/80	11/25/76	Albuminurea	Neg.	—

CIGARETTE SMOKING (Check one and complete as applicable.)

_____ never smoked   _____ ex-smoker   _____ present smoker   _____ Number per day/present

MEDICALLY DEFINED CONDITIONS: (Check either No or Yes column for each condition listed currently present. Also specify as indicated the information for each condition in the last two columns below whether or not currently present.)

Currently present?	No	Yes	Type/Location	Duration (yr./mo.)
Alcoholism			consumption/day _____ cirrhosis _____	
Anemia			Aplastic _____ B-12 _____ Folic acid _____ Sickle cell _____ Iron (Hg < 10 mg) _____	
Angina/MI			Angina _____ MI _____	
Arthritis			Osteo _____ Joint _____ Rheumatoid _____	
Cardiac arrhythmia			At.Fib _____ BBBlock L_____ R_____ HB_____ Complete _____ Incomplete _____	
Congest. Ht. Failure			Medication Diet	
Decub. ulcers			Site Size	
Diabetes mellitus			Insulin _____ - _____ - _____ dosage Other Diet	
Drug abuse			Specify drugs	
Hypertension		X	B.P. 160 / 80 Therapy	10 yrs.
Malignancy			Site Metastasis _____ Arrested _____	
Mental Illness			Psychosis _____ Anxiety _____ Depression _____	
Neuro. disorders		X	Specify rt. hemiplegia CVA	2 mos.
Respir. disease (chr.)			Asthma _____ Bronchitis _____ Emphysema _____	

NEAR NORTH PAVILION, ILLINOIS MASONIC MEDICAL CENTER
NURSING HISTORY

Date and Time of Evaluation ___ *2*___ AM (PM) *12 / 1 / 76*   **MRS. W.T.**
                                              Mo. Day Yr.   **AGE 80**

Date of Admission (or anticipated) *12 / 2 / 76*
                                    Mo. Day Yr.

Informant _*SISTER AND R.J., R.N.*_
          Patient or Other (Relationship)

SOCIO-DEMOGRAPHIC DATA

Religious Preference: _____ none   _____ Jewish   _____ other (specify)
                      __✓_ Catholic   _____ Protestant   _____

Race: __✓_ White   _____ Amer. Indian   _____ Chinese   _____ other (specify)
        _____ Black   _____ Japanese   _____ Filipino   _____

Patient Location   *Residential*   *Health Care Facility*
(present)
                    _____ private residence   _____ domicillary/personal care
                    _____ rented room (comm.)   _____ intermediate care
                    _____ apartment   _____ nursing home
Site of evaluation if different   _____ extended care
                                                  _____ chronic dis./rehab. hosp.
_____   _____ mental hospital
                                                  _____ other specialty hospital
                                                  __✓ short term acute hosp.

Length of time   If residential   If Health Care Facility
at Location   Specify date:
                   _____   This admission *10/16/76*
                   yrs./mos.   First admission_____

Living Arrangements   _____ own home   _____ alone
(ck. those that   __✓_ another's home   _____ with spouse
apply)   _____ paying   __✓_ with other, who *sister*
                            _____ not paying   _____ health related facil.
                            _____ rented room   _____(type)

Living Children — specify by number: sons __*0*___   daughters ___*0*___

Education   _____ college grad. (beyond baccalaureate)   __✓ high school diploma
            _____ undergrad. coll./degree   _____ trade, tech., voc. school
            __✓_ some undergrad./no degree   with h.s. diploma
            _____ trade, tech., voc. school   _____ 9-11 grades completed
                   no h.s. diploma   _____ 8 grades completed
            _____ no school   _____ fewer than 8 grades completed

Usual Occupation ____ Specify *Dept. Store*   or ck. _____ military   _____ housewife
       Retired Buyer   _____ never employed

SOCIO-DEMOGRAPHIC DATA (cont.)

Employment Status   ____ employed   ____ working, hrs/wk _____
                                     ____ rec. pay   ____ inside home/facility
                                     ✓ retired   ____ outside home/facility
                                     ____ unemployed   ✓ receiving pension
                                                         ____ never in labor market

Family Income   ____ less than $3,000   ____ $7,000-$9,999
(ck. one)   ____ $3,000-$4,999   ____ $10,000-$14,999
                               ____ $5,000-$6,999   ✓ $15,000 +

Health Care   ____ None   List other health insurance patient has.
Coverage   ✓ Medicare   (Specify below.)
                       ____ Medicaid   _____
                       ____ Workmen's comp.   _____

Hobbies/special interests *Knitting, crocheting, T.V., music*

Psychological Data

For oriented patients, describe the patient's adjustment to illness and new environment:

Describe patient's goals or objectives *Unable to set goals for*
(for care in nursing home) *herself at this time.*

Functioning Status

Mode of admission   ____ ambulatory   ____ w/c   ✓ stretcher   ____ other

General physical condition: *Poor*

Allergies: *None known*

NEAR NORTH PAVILION, ILLINOIS MASONIC MEDICAL CENTER *MRS. W.T.*
NURSING HISTORY (Continued) *AGE 80*

FUNCTIONAL ASSESSMENT

Mobility Level

Goes outside facility	Moves about facility	Confined
____ w/o help	____ w/o help	____ chair
____ with help, describe	✓ with help, describe	____ bed
	requires attendant	

Describe devices used _____

Transferring

Transfers | Does not Transfer | Describe devices used
____ w/o help `0` | ____ done by others `16` |
✓ with help, describe `4` | ____ bedfast |
attendant must hold rt. arm

Walking

Walks | Does not Walk | Describe devices used
____ w/o help `0` | ____ bedfast | *uses 4-point cane*
✓ with help, describe `16` | ____ chairfast | *(in left hand)*
needs attendant support rt. arm

Wheeling

Wheels | Does not wheel | Describe devices used
____ w/o help `0` | ____ walks |
____ with help, describe `4` | ____ chairfast |
 | ____ bedfast |
 | ✓ is wheeled by |
 | others `8` |

Stair Climbing

Goes up and down stairs | Does not climb stairs
____ w/o help `0` | ✓ goes up/down curb
✓ with help, describe `8` | ____ goes up/down one/two steps
 | ____ uses ramp for one/two steps
 | ____ uses elevator/chair lift

Describe devices used *See walking (above.)*

Bathing

Bathes | Where Bathed | Describe devices used
____ w/o help `0` | ✓ bed `20` | *Can be bathed*
____ with help, describe `18` | ____ sink `18` | *in tub*
_____ or | ✓ tub `18` |
✓ is bathed by others | ____ shower `18` |
(See next column.)

Dressing

Dresses | ✓ is dressed by others `30` | Kind of Dress
____ w/o help `0` | regularly (any clothes) | ____ street clothes only `5`
____ with help, describe | | ____ robe & PF/gown only `5`
See 3rd column. | | ____ slippers only `5`
 | | ____ shoes only `5`
 | | ____ 2 or more of above `20`

FUNCTIONAL ASSESSMENT (cont.)

Eating/Feeding

Eats
- ____ w/o help [0]
- ____ with help, describe [20]
- ________________

Where
- ____ bed
- ____ chair in room
- ____ dining room

Is Fed
- ____ orally by others [45]
- ✓ tube fed [45]
- ____ parentally fed [45]

Describe any devices used ________________

Toileting

Uses Toilet Room
- ____ w/o help [0]
- ✓ with help, describe [8]
- ________________

When
- ____ all the time
- ✓ day only
- ____ never

Substitutes
- night bedpan/urinal [8]
- ____ commode [8]

Describe any devices used ________________

Bowel Function
- ____ no problem [0]
- ____ impaction
- ✓ involuntary loss [18]
- ____ bowel training [18]

Ostomy
- ____ self care
- ____ not self care [18]

Describe devices used
diaper

Bladder Function
- ____ no problem [0]
- ____ retention
- ✓ involuntary loss [48]
- ____ bladder training [50]

- ____ ostomy
- ____ indwelling catheter [20]
- ____ external device
  describe

- ____ self care
- ____ not self care. [20]

Describe any devices used diaper

Orientation (Check one and complete as applicable.)
- ____ oriented [0]
- ✓ disoriented
- ____ comatose [36]

If disoriented, use the table to indicate by (x) the area(s) and frequency.

	Always [16]	or Part-Time [8]
Time	✓	
Place	✓	
Person		

Communication of needs (Check one and complete as applicable.)
- ✓ verbally [0]
- ____ nonverbally, specify how Occasionally unable or unwilling to talk [4]
- ____ does not communicate [8] (but not comatose)

NEAR NORTH PAVILION, ILLINOIS MASONIC MEDICAL CENTER
NURSING HISTORY (Continued)

MRS. W. T.

AGE 80

BEHAVIOR PATTERN

Check and complete as appropriate.

_____ appropriate behavior ⬛0️⃣

_____ inappropriate behavior

    _____ wandering, passive 1️⃣

    _____ abusive, aggressive 3️⃣

    _____ agitated 2️⃣

    ✔ hallucinating 2️⃣

    ✔ withdrawn 2️⃣

    ✔ depressed 2️⃣

_____ once a week or less 1️⃣

✔ more often than once a week 2️⃣

_____ able to follow instructions

6 ___ THIS COLUMN TOTAL X **2** THIS COLUMN TOTAL = **12**

Narrative exposition of frequent patterns:

When she is with a familiar person or a one-to-one basis she is cooperative and oriented. When she has been alone she has periods of withdrawl and is disoriented as to time and place. Occasionally hallucinates.

IMPAIRMENTS

Sight

_____ no impairment

_____ legally blind

_✓_ impairment, describe

_____

Type of compensation

_✓_ glasses

_____ contact lens

_____ large print

_____ other, describe _____

Hearing

_✓_ no impairment

_____ does not hear

_____ impairment, describe

_____

Type of compensation

_____ loud voices

_____ shouting

_____ hearing aid

_____ lip reading

_____ other, specify _____

Describe any devices used _____

Speech

_____ no impairment

_____ does not speak

_✓_ impairment, describe *speech slow at times Incoherent*

Type of compensation

_____ writes

_____ gestures

_____ sign language

_____ other, specify _____

Fractures and Dislocations

_✓_ none

_____ hip fracture

    _____ with prosthesis

    _____ with repair

_____ other fracture(s), describe

_____

_____ dislocation(s), describe

_____

Joint Motion

_____ no impairment

_✓_ impairment, use table to specify site joint and side(s) and check column for type

---

Joint site (R, L, B)	pain/ swelling	limited mobility	immobility	instability
ⓇR hand, all fingers		Spastic contracture		

See instructions — facing page

NEAR NORTH PAVILION, ILLINOIS MASONIC MEDICAL CENTER
NURSING HISTORY (Continued)

MRS. W. T.

AGE 80

IMPAIRMENTS (cont.)

Missing Limbs

✔ none missing

_____ missing, use table to specify missing part(s) and check column for prosthesis

Missing part(s)	Rt., left, both	Prosthesis

Paralysis

_____ none
✔ paralysis, describe type and location

spastic paralysis, (R) hand
unable to swallow

✔ muscular weakness, wasting or atrophy (R) *sided weakness*

Dentition

_____ no teeth missing
✔ some teeth missing
_____ edentulous
_____ special diet, describe

Type of compensation
✔ partial plate
_____ complete upper plate
_____ complete lower plate
_____ other appliances, describe

See instructions — facing page

Nursing Physical

The nurse is to examine the patient physically and note the pertinent findings. This is not meant to be a duplication of the physician's physical examination; it is an opportunity for the nurse to obtain first-hand knowledge of the patient's physical condition upon admission to the nursing home. Let us proceed to review the tool IMMC has adopted for use.

NEAR NORTH PAVILION, ILLINOIS MASONIC MEDICAL CENTER
NURSING PHYSICAL   *MRS. W.T.*
                                                    AGE 80
Including Review of Symptoms

Document assessments and observations of the following:

Component Observed	Additional Content that may be Recorded — Systemic Review
Vital Signs	
Blood Pressure	1. Systolic and Diastolic (R) arm *160 / 80*
	2. Systolic and Diastolic (L) arm *160 / 70*
Pulse	1. Quality: *Full*
	2. Rhythm: *regular*
	3. Rate: *70*
Respiration	1. Quality: *Normal*
	2. Rate: *20*
Weight	1. Compare to normal range for height (*63* in.) *110 lbs.*
EENT	
Eyes	1. Glaucoma, cataract
	2. Diploplia
	3. Infection
	4. Recent change
	5. * *No impairment noted*
Ears	1. Earaches
	2. Vertigo
	3. Discharge, infection
	4. *Normal*
Nose	1. Sinus pain
	2. Postnasal drip
	3. Epistaxis
	4. *Normal*

*Note: Additional spaces left for other positive findings.

Component Observed	Additional Content that may be Recorded — Systemic Review

EENT (Cont.)

Throat
1. Toothache
2. Bleeding, cracked lips
3. Gums, mouth, tongue
4. Hoarseness
5. *Gag reflex present (does not swallow food)*

Poor oral hygiene, gums appear infected, thick dried mucous roof of mouth

Neck
1. Limitation of motion
2.
3.

Neck stiff to flexion, extension and rotation. Will not swallow when requested.

Chest

Lungs
1. Dyspnea
2. Orthopnea
3. Wheezes, rales *slight, lower left lobe*
4.

Heart
1. Apical-Radial Pulse *70 / 70*
2. Palpitation
3. *No murmurs*
4.

Breasts
1. Discharge
2. Pain *Normal*
3. Mass
4.

Abdomen
1. Mass *Normal*
2. Hernia (truss?) *None*
3. *Normal*
4.

Genitalia
1. Discharge, odor
2. Pap smear
3. *Good hygiene*
4.

Rectum
1. Hemorrhoids *None*
2. Fecal impaction *None*
3.
4.

Extremities
1. Varicose veins
2. Thrombophlebitis
3. Range of motion capability *(R) hand, fingers contracted spastic, but can be completely extended*
4. Joint swelling
5.
6. *Right side weakness all arm + leg muscles.*

Skin
1. Color *pale*
2. Tone, turgor *dry*
3. Lesions *None*
4. If decubiti, location and measure width and depth. *None, but slight redness of skin over coccyx*

Problem List

Instructions to Learner:

Using the data supplied on the previous assessment forms, prepare your own problem list using the format found on page 103, chapter 12. Then compare your list with the problem list below developed by Jane Roe, R.N. at Near North Pavilion on this page.

NEAR NORTH PAVILION, ILLINOIS MASONIC MEDICAL CENTER **MRS. W.T.**
PROBLEM LIST **AGE 80**

Problem #	Active Problem	Onset Date	Resolve Date	Potential Problem	Eval. Date
1.	Inability to Swallow	10/16/76			
2.	ⓇL side muscle weakness	10/16/76			
3.	Confusion	On admission 12/2			
4.	Poor oral hygiene	12/2			
5.	Incontinent Bladder	10/16			
6.	Bowel	10/16			
7.				skin breakdown over coccyx	daily

Nursing Actions

Instructions to Learner:

Complete a separate nursing actions form for each problem you have identified. Do this for at least six problems. Use a facsimile of the form found on page 105, chapter 12. Then compare your goals, objectives, and nursing actions for each problem with those developed by Jane Roe, R.N., which appear immediately following.

NEAR NORTH PAVILION, ILLINOIS MASONIC MEDICAL CENTER
NURSING ACTIONS FOR PROBLEM NUMBER ①

(Use separate sheet for *each* problem on problem list.)

MRS. W.T.
AGE 80

Problem: Unable to swallow (due to stroke.) Date of Onset 10/16/76   Date Resolved ☐

Immediate Outcome (goals): Ability to take food and swallow without choking (eliminate need for gastrostomy)

Date to be accomplished/reevaluated: 1 month (1/2/77)

Intermediate Outcome (objectives)	By what date	Specific nursing action (if prn, state circumstances)	Date begin	Time/frequency	Who performs	Evaluation who/frequency
Maintain adequate nutrition and fluid balance		① Gastrostomy feeding per M.D. order	12/2	q 6 hrs	RN or LPN	RN/weekly
Regain ability to swallow		② Offer small amounts of water P.O.	12/2	q 3 hrs	RN	RN/daily
		③ Encourage her to eat by taking her to D.R. at mealtime	12/4	at meal time	Aide	RN/weekly

Nursing actions should be transferred to "Nursing Action Order Card" (Kardex) and noted at that time.

For patient classification—nursing action guideline used for this problem ☑

Jane Roe, R.N.
Nurse's Signature/Title

NEAR NORTH PAVILION, ILLINOIS MASONIC MEDICAL CENTER
NURSING ACTIONS FOR PROBLEM NUMBER ②

(Use separate sheet for *each* problem on problem list.)

MRS. W.T.
AGE 80

Problem ® sided muscle weakness (due to stroke)   Date of Onset 10/16/76   Date Resolved ☐

Immediate Outcome (goals) Normal muscle function ® side

Date to be accomplished/reevaluated 1 month (1/2/77)

Intermediate Outcome (objectives)	By what date	Specific nursing action (if prn, state circumstances)	Date begin	Time/frequency	Who performs	Evaluation who/frequency
Restore full range of motion all joints right hand	12/16	① R.O.M. exercises	12/2	tid	nurse-tech.	P.T./weekly
	1/2/77	② Resistance extension exercises ®hand and other weak muscles	12/2	bid	P.T.	P.T./weekly
Increase strength of muscles	1/2/77	③ walk in walker (see ®)	12/2	qid	Nurse tech.	P.T./weekly
		④ knitting	12/2	bid	O.T. tech	O.T./weekly

Nursing actions should be transferred to "Nursing Action Order Card" (Kardex) and noted at that time.

For patient classification—nursing action guideline used for this problem ☑

Jane Roe, R.N.

Nurse's Signature/Title

NEAR NORTH PAVILION, ILLINOIS MASONIC MEDICAL CENTER
NURSING ACTIONS FOR PROBLEM NUMBER ③

(Use separate sheet for *each* problem on problem list.)

MRS. W. T
AGE 80

Problem _Mental confusion_

Immediate Outcome (goals) _Normal orientation to time, place, person_

Date of Onset _12/2_ On admission

Date Resolved

Date to be accomplished/reevaluated _12/16_

Intermediate Outcome (objectives)	By what date	Specific nursing action (if prn, state circumstances)	Date begin	Time/ frequency	Who performs	Evaluation who/frequency
Same as goal	12/16	① Reality orientation	constant		all personnel	charge nurse weekly
		② Assign one nurse tech. for all bedside care				
		a) Talk to patient while providing all care				
		b) Talk slowly when giving directions				
		c) encourage dining room				
		d) encourage activities				

Nursing actions should be transferred to "Nursing Action Order Card" (Kardex) and noted at that time.

For patient classification—nursing action guideline used for this problem ③

Jane Doe, R.N.
Nurse's Signature/Title

NEAR NORTH PAVILION, ILLINOIS MASONIC MEDICAL CENTER

MRS. W.T.
AGE 80

NURSING ACTIONS FOR PROBLEM NUMBER ___②___

(Use separate sheet for *each* problem on problem list.)

Problem _Poor oral hygiene_   Date of Onset: On admission 12/2

Immediate Outcome (goals) _Normal oral mucous membranes_

Date Resolved ☐

Date to be accomplished/reevaluated _12/9_

Intermediate Outcome (objectives)	By what date	Specific nursing action (if prn, state circumstances)	Date begin	Time/frequency	Who performs	Evaluation who/frequency
Remove secretions	12/4	Special mouth care (Remove + clean partial plate)	12/2	tid	Nurse tech.	Charge nurse/g 8 days
				"		"
Patient to maintain good mouth care	12/9	Teach brushing + use of mouth wash	12/4	tid p.c.	Nurse tech	Charge nurse/ weekly
Maintain humid environment		Humidifier at bedside	12/2			Charge nurse/ weekly

Nursing actions should be transferred to "Nursing Action Order Card" (Kardex) and noted at that time.

For patient classification—nursing action guideline used for this problem ☐ 3

Jane Roe, R.N.
Nurse's Signature/Title

NEAR NORTH PAVILION, ILLINOIS MASONIC MEDICAL CENTER
NURSING ACTIONS FOR PROBLEM NUMBER _⑤_   MRS. W. T.
     AGE 80

(Use separate sheet for *each* problem on problem list.)

Problem _Bladder Incontinence_

Immediate Outcome (goals) _Control of urination_

	Date of Onset	On admission 12/2			Date Resolved ☐

Intermediate Outcome (objectives)	By what date	Specific nursing action (if prn, state circumstances)	Date begin	Time/ frequency	Date to be accomplished/ reevaluated 1/2/77	
					Who performs	Evaluation who/frequency
Same	1/2/77	Routine bladder continence training	12/2	Per routine procedure	Nurse tech.	Charge nurse/ weekly

Nursing actions should be transferred to "Nursing Action Order Card" (Kardex) and noted at that time.

For patient classification—nursing action guideline used for this problem ☑

Jane Roe, R.N.
Nurse's Signature/Title

NEAR NORTH PAVILION, ILLINOIS MASONIC MEDICAL CENTER
NURSING ACTIONS FOR PROBLEM NUMBER _6_

(Use separate sheet for *each* problem on problem list.)

Problem _Bowel Incontinence_   MRS. W.T.
                                      AGE 80

Immediate Outcome (goals) _Normal bowel function with_
continence

Date of Onset _12/2_ On admission
Date Resolved

Intermediate Outcome (objectives)	By what date	Specific nursing action (if prn, state circumstances)	Date begin	Time/ frequency	Who performs	Date to be accomplished/ reevaluated	Evaluation who/frequency
Same	1/2/97	Routine bowel control training	12/2	See routine procedure	Nurse tech.	1/2/97	Charge nurse / weekly

Nursing actions should be transferred to "Nursing Action Order Card" (Kardex) and noted at that time.

For patient classification—nursing action guideline used for this problem ☐ B

Jane Roe, R.N.
Nurse's Signature/Title

NEAR NORTH PAVILION, ILLINOIS MASONIC MEDICAL CENTER
NURSING ACTIONS FOR PROBLEM NUMBER ___*(7)*___

(Use separate sheet for *each* problem on problem list.)

Problem _*Potential skin breakdown (coccyx)*_   Date of Onset ___—___

MRS. W.T.
AGE 80

Immediate Outcome (goals) _*Prevent skin breakdown*_

Date Resolved
☐   Date to be accomplished/reevaluated

Intermediate Outcome (objectives)	By what date	Specific nursing action (if prn, state circumstances)	Date begin	Time/frequency	Who performs	Evaluation who/frequency
Same		*Special back care (see procedures manual)*	10/12	*bid*	*Nurse tech.*	*Charge nurse/weekly*

Nursing actions should be transferred to "Nursing Action Order Card" (Kardex) and noted at that time.

For patient classification—nursing action guideline used for this problem [3]

Jane Roe R.N.
Nurse's Signature/Title

Patient Classification

Instructions to Learner:

Using data supplied in the physician's care plan, nursing history and physical, and your nursing actions for six problems, you should be able to complete a patient classification form using the sample forms found on pages 124-131. Compare your classification with that performed by Jane Roe, R.N., which appears immediately following.

NEAR NORTH PAVILION, ILLINOIS MASONIC MEDICAL CENTER
PATIENT CLASSIFICATION

MRS. W.T.

Based on following component of patient assessment: *AGE 80*

1. Physician's Care Plan

    A. Medical status: Risk Factor Measurements

        1. Compare height and weight with standard tables (M/F)
            Rate 1 unit for each 10 lbs. overweight

            COMPUTATION:

            Ht. **63"** Wt. **110** lbs. overweight $\dfrac{0}{10}$ =   **0**

            EXAMPLE: Ht. 6'0" Wt. 219 Lbs. overweight $\dfrac{39}{10}$ =   **4**

        2. Blood pressure
            Rate 1 unit for each 20 mm Hg. over 130 systolic
            Rate 1 unit for each 10 mm Hg. over 80 diastolic

            COMPUTATION:

            Systolic BP **160** mm Hg − 130 = $\dfrac{30}{20}$ =   **7**

            Diastolic BP **80** mm Hg − 80 = $\dfrac{0}{10}$ =   **0**

            EXAMPLE:

            Systolic BP 156 mm Hg − 130 = $\dfrac{26}{20}$ =   **1**

            Diastolic BP 100 mm Hg − 80 = $\dfrac{20}{10}$ =   **2**

        3. Blood cholesterol (mg %) **200**   **0**
            Rate 1 unit if over 300 mg%
            Rate "0" if under 300 mg%

        4. Albuminuria (0 to 4 +)
            Rate 1 unit for every 2 + result

            COMPUTATION:

            Albuminuria $\dfrac{0}{2}$ **0**

            EXAMPLES:
                  $\dfrac{1+}{2} = 0;$ $\dfrac{3+}{2} = 1$

NEAR NORTH PAVILION, ILLINOIS MASONIC MEDICAL CENTER
PATIENT CLASSIFICATION (Continued)   *MRS. W. T.*
                                                       AGE 80

    5. Cigarette Smoking
       Present smoker (cigarettes/day) _____*0*_____ /day
       Rate 1 unit for each *pack* of cigarettes smoked/day.

       COMPUTATION:

       $$\frac{\text{Cigarettes smoked/day}}{20} \qquad = \boxed{0}$$

       EXAMPLE:
              $$\text{Cigarettes smoked/day} \quad \frac{50}{20} \qquad = \square$$

---

1. Physician's Care Plan
   A. Risk Factors

                                      Sub-total units $\boxed{1}$ 1.A.

   B. Medically Defined Conditions

       Rate 1 unit of *each* of the currently present
       diseases specified in list.   Sub-total units $\boxed{2}$ 1.B.

2. Nursing History and Physical

   A. Functioning status

      1. Mobility level
         Classify patient as basically
         Bed patient _____
         Chair patient _____
         Ambulatory __✓__
         Assign appropriate units on functional status summary sheet on reverse of this
         page.

      2. Others
         Refer to Nursing History, "Functional Status" evaluation. For each functional
         (transferring, walking, wheeling, etc.) level checked which has an assigned
         weight unit $\boxed{\text{No.}}$

         place appropriate units in boxes $\square$ on Functional

         Status Summary sheet on reverse of this page.

   B. Impairments

       Rate 1 unit for each impairment identified *for which the patient has not compen-
       sated* to "normal" function.

                           TOTAL UNITS $\boxed{2}$ 2.B.

FUNCTIONAL STATUS SUMMARY

MRS. W.T. AGE 90

FUNCTIONARY STATUS	BED PATIENT	CHAIR	AMBULATORY	PATIENT RATING UNITS
Mobility Level	36	8	0	0
Transferring	NA	0 , 4 or 16	0 or 4	4
Walking	NA	16	0 or 16	16
Wheeling	NA	0 , 4 or 8	0 , 4 or 8	8
Stair Climbing	NA	0 or 8	0 or 8	8
Bathing	20	0 , 18 or 20	0 or 18	18
Dressing	NA	0 , 5 , 20 or 30	0 , 5 , 20 or 30	30
Eating/Feeding	0 , 20 or 45	0 , 20 or 45	0 , 20 or 45	45
Toileting	0* or 8**	0 or 8	0 or 8	8
Bowel Function	0 or 18	0 or 18	0 or 18	18
Bladder Function	0 , 20 , 48 or 50	0 , 20 , 48 or 50	0 , 20 , 48 or 50	50
Orientation	0 , 8 , 16 or 36	0 , 8 or 16	0 , 8 or 16	16
Communication of Needs	0 , 4 or 8	0 , 4 or 8	0 , 4 or 8	4
Behavior	0 to 24	0 to 24	0 to 24	24
TOTAL UNITS				**233**

2.A.

*Bed patient with bowel and/or bladder dysfunction (see next two items).
**Bed patient using bed pan/urinal with no bowel or bladder dysfunction.

NEAR NORTH PAVILION, ILLINOIS MASONIC MEDICAL CENTER
PATIENT CLASSIFICATION (Continued)   *MRS. W.T.*

Based on following component of patient assessment: *AGE 80*

3. Nursing Actions

    A. For *each problem* identified, rate units according to goals (imediate outcome) and restorative potential.

        5 units for each problem in which the goal is restoration to maximum potential.

        1 unit for each problem in which the goal is only maintenance.

        In this classification system, nursing actions are not weighted for more than 6 problems. Therefore, the patient's 6 most important problems should be selected for this classification of nursing actions. Use the *same* problems for rating nursing actions under parts A and B. (Refer to Classification Summary sheet, page 130.)

        [30] 3.A.

    B. For *each problem*, rate *specific* nursing actions ordered for *any objective* (intermediate outcome) according to the following guidelines. For each of the seven guidelines that follow, consider all specific nursing actions to determine which guideline applies, 1 through 7; rate only *once* for each *problem* in rank order; rate for guideline 1, if applicable, before using guideline 2; guideline 2 before guideline 3; etc.

Guideline 1. Nursing action requiring *procedure* to be *performed* by an RN (skilled nursing procedure). (Includes RN evaluation.)

    15 units if performed daily   X _*2*_ * = *30*

    5 units if performed 3 times a week   X ____* =

    3 units if performed less than 3 times a week   X ____* = _____
                                                                         Sum

                                                            [30] 3.B.1

Guideline 2. Nursing action requiring *judgment* of an RN (skilled nursing supervision) as to where and if a PRN medication (other than laxatives, HS sedation, non-prescription meds) is given, a procedure performed, or patient observed for development of a specific potential problem that appears on the problem list. (Includes RN evaluation.)

    15 units if required daily   X ____* =

    5 units if required 3 times a week   X ____* =

    3 units if required less than 3 times a week   X ____* = _____
                                                                         Sum

                                                            [ ] 3.B.2.

*Total problems for which guideline applies.

NEAR NORTH PAVILION, ILLINOIS MASONIC MEDICAL CENTER
PATIENT CLASSIFICATION (Continued)   *M RS. W. T.*

Based on following component of patient assessment: *AGE 80*

Guideline 3. Nursing action requiring *evaluation* by an RN (skilled nursing supervision/evaluation)

    10 units if required daily   X _____ * =

    5 units if required 3 times a week   X _*1*_ * = *5*

    3 units if required less than 3 times a week   X _*3*_ * = *9*

                                               Sum

                                       [14] 3.B.3.

Nursing action requiring a procedure to be performed by nursing personnel other than an RN (non-skilled nursing procedure). Do not include any non-skilled nursing actions that would duplicate rating for care provided for functional disabilities (previously rated on page 126).

NOTE: 1, 2, and 3 above also apply to skilled professional services provided by a *physical therapist, speech therapist* and/or *clinical psychologist.*

Guideline 4. Nursing action (non-skilled) requiring standard nursing procedures (see procedure book) (such as routine back care).

    3 units if performed daily   X _____ * =

    1 unit if performed 3 times a week   X _____ * = _____

                                               Sum

                                       [ ] 3.B.4.

Guideline 5. Nursing action (non-skilled) requiring a variation from standard or routine nursing procedures (see procedure book) (such as crush all medications, special back care, etc.).

    5 units if required daily   X _____ * =

    2 units if required 3 times a week   X _____ * =

    1 unit if required less than 3 times a week X _____ * = _____

                                               Sum

                                           3.B.5.

Guideline 6. Nursing action requiring orientation therapy

    3 units   X _____ = [ ] 3.B.6

Guideline 7. Other attitudinal therapy.

    3 units   X _____ = [ ] 3.B.7

                                  TOTAL
                                  ALL PROBLEMS [14]

*Total problems for which guide applies.

NEAR NORTH PAVILION, ILLINOIS MASONIC MEDICAL CENTER
PATIENT CLASSIFICATION (Continued) *MRS. W.T.*
AGE 80

4. Evaluation of appropriate level of care

[✓] Skilled nursing level. This level is justified if:

    1. An RN is required to *perform daily* a skilled nursing procedure (nursing action guideline 1).

    2. An RN is required to make skilled nursing *judgments daily* (nursing action guideline 2).

    3. An RN is required to *evaluate daily* non-skilled tasks and procedures performed by others (nursing action guideline 3).

    4. An RN is required to do one of 1, 2, or 3 (above) every other day *and* another skilled professional is providing rehabilitation services on the alternate days (physical therapist, speech therapist, occupational therapist [*therapeutic only; not diversional*], clinical psychologist, psychiatric social worker).

[ ] Intermediate care level. This level is justified if patient is receiving care as identified in No. 1 through No. 4 under skilled nursing, but *not on a daily basis*.

[ ] Custodial care. This level is justified if maintenance is only goal and no specific nursing actions are required.

(Check appropriate level on summary sheet.)

5. DNS statement of level of care.
(Initial Utilization Review certification)
I believe, based on the foregoing documentation of nursing care needs of
_____*MRS. W.T.*_____ that he/she requires_____
    (Patient)
_____*skilled*_____ level of care for at least
    (Level specification)
___*30*___ days. The patient's continued need for this level of care will be reevaluated
    (number)
by the Utilization Review Committee on _____*1/2/77*_____
    (date)
_*12/2/76*_ (Date) _*Jane Doe, R.N.*_____ RN, DNS
Approved by Utilization Committee

_____
    Chairman, UR Committee

_____
    Date

The Utilization Review Committee disagrees with the assessment and declares a
_____ level of care is required. The patient's continued need will be
reevaluated on _____.
    (date)
_____ Chairman, UR Committee _____ Date

_____ Medical Director _____ Date

_____ Nursing Home Administrator _____ Date

PATIENT CARE CLASSIFICATION SUMMARY   NEAR NORTH PAVILION, ILLINOIS MASONIC MEDICAL CENTER

Patient __MRS. W.T.__   Patient Number _____
__AGE 80__

Data Source	Evaluation Elements	Initial Evaluation Total Units (date)	Subsequent Evaluations Units (date)	Units (date)	Units (date)	Units (date)
Physician's Care Plan	A. Risk Factors	1 (12/2/76)				
	B. Current Diseases	2				
Nursing History and Physical	A. Functional Status	235				
	B. Impairments	2				

Use these blocks on subsequent evaluations to note problem numbers of problems *rated*. (See problem list.) Also note total number of *active* problems as of this date.

Nursing Actions

# of Problem Rated (See Problem List)	A. Goal/Units (Restorative = 5) (Maintenance = 1) for Problem Rated	B. Specific Actions Check (x) Guideline Which Applies							Units
		1	2	3	4	5	6	7	
1. ⓪	5	✓							15
2. ②	5	✓	✓						15
3. 3	5			✓					3
4. ⑦	5			✓					3
5. ⑤	5			✓					3
6. ⑥									
Total Units									44
Total # of Active Problems **7**	**Total Units/Goals**							30	30

Initial Evaluation Total Units: 44, 30

Level of Care	
Skilled	✓
Intermediate	
Custodial	

TOTAL POINTS (Add All Evaluation Units)   317

On this sheet enter totals from appropriate ☐ from evaluation summary

NEAR NORTH PAVILION, ILLINOIS MASONIC MEDICAL CENTER
ANALYSIS OF PATIENT CARE REQUIREMENTS AS OF _____12/2/76_____ (date)

Patient Name	Pat. No.	Room No.	# of Problems	Care Level*	Total Points =	Physician's Care Plan		Nursing History & Physical		Nursing Actions		Remarks
						Risk Factors +	Current Diseases +	Functional Status +	Impairments +	Goal (Restorative Potential) +	Total Units	
MRS. W.T.	1076	702	7	S	314	1	2	235	8	30	44	Requires 314/60 = 5¼ hrs. training care per day ← approximated minutes of Rtl time/day (remainder) non-R.N. nursing pers./day

Total
Points

* Note Code
S = Skilled   C = Custodial
I = Intermediate   R = Residential

Appendix C

Other Classification Systems in Use for Long Term Care

Examples of two other classification systems currently in use are provided in this appendix. The first of these classifications systems is that developed by William Thoms, Regional Director, First Healthcare Corporation, for use at Greenbriar Terrace Healthcare, Nashua, New Hampshire. The weights assigned in the Greenbriar system represent minutes of nursing time required to perform certain nursing tasks and procedures. The sum of total units represents the minutes of nursing time that must be devoted to a specific patient on a daily basis. Mrs. W. T., whose patient care plan appears in Appendix B, has also been classified according to the Thoms classification system.

The second classification system is that currently employed by the Department of Public Health of Illinois. The points in this classification system do *not* represent minutes of nursing time required. They have been arbitrarily set, but reimbursement does vary with the total points. Patients with 25 points or more in this system are identified as requiring a skilled level of care. Mrs. W. T., whose patient care plan is found in Appendix B, has also been classified according to this system.

GREENBRIAR TERRACE HEALTH CARE

Line Item Instructions for the Completion of the Patient Care Profile Form

1. Patient name: self explanatory
2. Patient number: State medical number or if the patient does not have one, his Social Security number.

3. Room number
4. Facility's name
5. Facility State Provider number
6. Dispense meds and chart:
    Pouring, delivering, and charting medications; entering in nursing notes, misc. brief services including injections and vital signs that must be taken in conjunction with various medications.

7. Skilled observation daily: (note type)
    Any recorded observation specifically ordered in writing by a physician and performed by a professional nurse; i.e., apical pulses, neurological signs, B/P & TPR over and above any vital signs that might be taken as a prerequisite with certain medications.
    EXAMPLE: Can claim apical pulses taken qid on a patient with history of cardiac arrythmias.

8. Skilled procedure daily: (note type)
    a. Two or less separate types daily: Any procedure specifically ordered by a physician in writing that must be performed by a professional nurse; example: dressing change, tube feedings, catheter irrigation, eye and ear irrigations, IVs and clysis. (A single procedure done more than once daily constitutes only one procedure; for example: dressings tid counts as one procedure.)
    b. More than two separate types of procedures daily: Check this block also. Note: Multiple decubiti are considered as one procedure only.

9. Personal Hygiene:
    Nursing procedure by staff to maintain personal cleanliness and good grooming which includes attending and/or assisting with tub or shower bath, shaving, brushing teeth. (Cannot claim bed bath also.)

10. Bed Bath:
    Bath in room. (Cannot claim ' aid bathing'' also.) Completed entirely by nursing staff without assistance from patient.

11. Aid Dressing:
    Patient cannot dress and undress without assistance and is regularly helped.

12. Assist with Walking:
    Patient can bear own weight but must be assisted to a standing position, steadied and guided. Include wheelchair patients who cannot move or transfer alone (example: amputees, pivot transfers, hoyer lift).

13. Assist Eating:
    Can bring food to mouth, but requires special preparation, guidance or frequent encouragement to maintain proper diet. (Cannot claim "feed" also.)

14. Feed:
    Patient cannot inject food without constant assistance. Include tube feedings, clysis and IVs in this category also. (Cannot claim with "assist eating.")

15. Indwelling Catheter:
    Prescribed by a physician. Includes insertion, maintenance, catheter care and irrigation if less than once daily. (Cannot claim if patient is on clamping procedure for bladder training.)

16. Incontinence:
    Regular, daily incontinence due to patient's inability to control micturation or bowels or to notify staff of need. (Cannot claim if patient is on a bowel or bladder training program.) Also same person whose continence is maintained only through regular staff assistance in advance of need.

17. Bowel Incontinence with Foley Catheter:
    Patient with foley catheter who has regular, daily incontinence due to patient's inability to control bowels or to notify staff of need. (Cannot claim if patient is on a bowel training program.)

18. Bladder Training Program:
    A planned and documented program designed to reduce incontinence of urine. (Include clamping procedure for bladder training here.)

19. Bowel Training Program:

    A planned and documented program designed to reduce incontinence of feces. Also, patient with enemas prescribed routinely every 3 days or more frequently.

20. Turn in Bed:

    Patient essentially helpless to assist self and must be frequently positioned while in bed. Also include patients that require repositioning every two hours while up in the chair.

21. Decubitus Prevention:

    Allowance for extra attention (over and above ordinary back and skin care) to pressure points, active decubiti or patients with a past history of decubitus ulcers requiring constant skin surveillance.

22. Special Attention Required Due To:

    1. Disoriented wandering or fully ambulatory patients.
    2. Excessive overweight—to the point where much extra care is involved; for example: a very obese person who requires more frequent bathing, etc. to prevent intertrigenous area from breaking down or someone so heavy and helpless that it takes more than two people to change or position the patient.
    3. Severe spasticity or rigidity from fusions or locked joints caused by contractures or severe arthritis. Can claim this only if the problem is of such magnitude that it badly inhibits their care or ambulation.
    4. Patients that are so noisy that they require frequent attention to quiet them. This can only be claimed if all, well-documented efforts have been made to eliminate the cause for the patient's behavior.

Add 10% of items 6 through 21 if any or all of these conditions under SPECIAL ATTENTION REQUIRED are checked.

23. Restorative Nursing Care:

    Must be ordered by a physician in writing. Implementation of various types of patient re-teaching conducted daily by nursing staff. Must be well documented. For example, ADL, ostomy teaching, diabetic teaching or ambulation and range of motion after an illness that required re-learning such as fractured hips, CVAs, etc. Can only be claimed for the limited time necessary to affect the stated objective or to prove it impractical.

GREENBRIAR TERRACE HEALTHCARE

PATIENT CARE PROFILE

1. Patient's Name __*Mrs. W.T.*__
2. Patient's No. ___
3. Room No. ___
4. Facility Name ___
5. State Provider No. ___

.SERVICE — *12/2*

	SERVICE	TIME						
6.	Dispense meds and chart	30	30					
7.	Skilled observation daily	15	15					
8.	Skilled procedure daily:							
	a. 2 or less procedures daily	20	20					
	b. More than 2 procedures daily	15	15					
9.	Personal hygiene (assist)	18	—					
10.	Bed bath	20	20					
11.	Aid dressing	30	30					
12.	Aid walking	32	32					
13.	Assist eating	20	—					
14.	Feed	45	45					
15.	In-dwelling catheter	20	—					
16.	Incontinence	48	—					
17.	Bowel incontinence w/catheter	18	—					
18.	Bladder training	50	50					
19.	Bowel training	18	18					
20.	Turn in bed	36	—					
21.	Decubitus prevention	10	10					
		Total	285					
22.	Special attention required: Disoriented and wandering. Excessive overweight Rigidity of back extremities Add 10% of total, items 6-21	10%	—					
23.	Restorative nursing care	30	30					
		GRAND TOTAL	315					

Signature of Evaluator __*Jane Foe, R.N.*__ Date __*12/2/76*__

STATE OF ILLINOIS
Guidelines for Evaluation of Need for Care

The following guidelines are to be used by Department staff to determine point allowances and evaluate the need for care in group care facilities. Points are given, in each area of services below, on the basis of the highest level of services required and received by a recipient during the evaluation period. Points are allowed only for services provided by staff of the facility unless otherwise specified, as in the two point allowance in item 11. Points are not allowed for services recipients perform themselves or for services performed by individuals not employed by the facility, except where otherwise specified for individual items.

The evaluation is to be based on consultation with or written orders from the physician, personal observation of the recipient, and the facilities' record of services provided. In some instances casework staff are required to refer cases to the Regional Medical Assistance Consultant before allowing points or determining placement. Regional consultants are free to contact Regional Public Health Nurses, Department of Mental Health staff, or other professional medical or nursing personnel for consultation as needed.

A pound sign (#) in the criteria identified services which require care in a skilled nursing facility. In addition, a recipient having a total point count of 25 points or more, on a continuing basis, requires skilled care. An asterisk (*) identifies services which require care in an intermediate care facility. Services not identified by either a pound sign or an asterisk may be provided in sheltered care facilities. Before authorizing care in a group care facility, an evaluation of other, more suitable, arrangements for care must be investigated. Care in a group care facility is to be approved only when there is no appropriate alternative.

1. *Eating*

    0 — No point is allowed when the recipient is able to eat independently.

    1 — One point is allowed when the recipient requires assistance in cutting food, buttering bread, placing utensils for blind recipient, etc.

2 — Two points are allowed when the recipient requires and receives some individual assistance in eating from a staff member. The assistance may vary from complete feeding on some days to partial feeding on others. Also included here is the type of assistance which can be given by a staff member to more than one patient in the same room during the meal.

4 — Four points are allowed when the recipient requires and receives complete individual attention by a staff member at all meals. The staff member remains in constant attendance at the patient's side throughout mealtime to hand feed the recipient or to insure adequate intake of food.

8 — Eight points are allowed when the recipient is unable to take food by mouth and tube feeding or gastrostomy feeding are given by licensed nurses on the physician's orders.

2. *Mobility*

0 — No point is allowed then the recipient is independent in movement with or without assistive devices and no assistance is needed to enable him to move from place to place. This includes the recipient who is able to transfer himself to and from a wheelchair.

*2 — Two points are allowed when the recipient is able to move about but needs a staff member to assist him to get into a wheelchair, to begin walking with the walker; or to walk beside him to give assistance, etc.

May be allowed in a sheltered care facility for a recipient who can move about independently but needs assistance to get into a wheelchair or begin walking with a walker if (1) the facility is determined safe for the resident by the Illinois Department of Public Health (IDPH), (2) the resident's quarters are on the first floor, and (3) access to the facility is at grade level or ramps are provided. Prior approval is required from the Regional Medical Assistance Consultant who will verify safety with IDPH.

*3 — Three points are allowed when the recipient is unable to move about under his own power. He must be moved by a staff member. This may consist of pushing the wheelchair or lifting the patient. This also includes the recipient who is able to move except that his size or other physical condition requires that more than one nursing staff member be at his side to give assistance in moving about.

3. *Behavior or Mental Condition*

0 — No point is allowed for the recipient who is usually able to act in a manner that takes into account his needs and the needs of others and staff. He can be reasoned with and can adjust his behavior. On the whole, his behavior is consistently cooperative. He is aware of who he is and what is expected of him within the home. He does not require any special supervision.

3 — Three points are allowed for the recipient who requires occasional supervision from a staff member. He presents problems such as periods of hyperactivity or confusion, occasional strong reactions to frustrations or disappointments, prolonged periods of silence, excessive pacing or sleeping, or inability or unwillingness to interact. During such "ups and downs" he requires temporary support and vigilance from the staff.

*8 — Eight points are allowed for the recipient who requires special and continuous supervision by a licensed nurse. His tolerance is so low and unpredictable that a licensed nurse must be present in the facility at all times.

4. *Current Physical Rehabilitation Needs*

Rehabilitation nursing consists of services ordered by a physician, such as range of motion exercises, positioning, transfer activities, gait training, parallel bars, pulleys, and training of the aphasic. Bowel and bladder training programs are not included. The acute illnesses and injuries for which 8 or 12 points may be given include fractures of hip. pelvis, and extremities; acute brain trauma (to include spinal cord injuries or neurological disorders, but not to in-

clude congenital brain disorders); cerebral vascular accidents with resulting aphasia and/or hemiplegia; amputees
requiring pre- and post-prosthetic care and training.

0 — No point is allowed for the recipient who does not require rehabilitation or who has no potential for
rehabilitation.

*4 — Four points are allowed for the recipient who needs
and is receiving rehabilitation nursing services, performed or supervised by a licensed nurse, to maintain
current level of function.

*8 — Eight points are allowed for the recipient who needs
and is receiving rehabilitation nursing services performed or supervised by a licensed nurse, following
selected acute illnesses or injuries, to improve his level
of functioning, for a period from three to six months
following discharge from a hospital or rehabilitation
facility, *if the facility has an approved rehabilitation
nursing program.*

*12 — Twelve points are allowed for a recipient who needs
and is receiving intensive rehabilitation nursing services supervised by a licensed nurse following selected
acute illnesses or injuries within a period of three
months following discharge from a hospital or
rehabilitation facility, *if the facility has an approved
rehabilitation nursing program.*

5. *Catheterization (including irrigations)*

0 — No point is allowed when the recipient does not require
catheterization or irrigation.

*4 — Four points are allowed when the recipient requires an
occasional catheterization for a specimen or treatment,
or an indwelling catheter for a short term physical condition.

*8 — Eight points are allowed when the physician orders a
retention catheter to be used continuously. This also
includes full care of the catheter and irrigations.

When a retention catheter is used the patient shall not
be considered to be requiring or receiving care because
of bladder incontinence under item 6, even though in

some instances the patient may be on a bowel and bladder training program for a short period while the catheter is used.

6. *Incontinence (Bladder and Bowel)*

0 — No point is allowed when the recipient has complete bladder and bowel control.

1 — One point is allowed when recipient usually has control except on those infrequent occasions when he has an accident due to nervousness or visitors, or reaction to medications, such as cathartics.

2 — Two points are allowed when recipient is neither continent nor incontinent; sometimes he has control; other times he has none.

*8 — Eight points are allowed for a recipient who needs and is receiving services to maintain bowel or bladder control following a bowel and bladder training program.

*6 — Six points are allowed when the recipient has no bladder and/or bowel control and he requires care for cleanliness or comfort. This includes the patient who dribbles constantly.

*8 — Eight points are allowed when the recipient has in the past had no control but is now receiving training through an active bowel and bladder program. The physician has ordered such a program and the nursing care plan for the patient includes this program (maximum length of time—initial period three months; if successful an additional three months; maximum total six months).

7. *Douches, Enemas and/or Colostomy Irrigations*

0 — No point is allowed when recipient does not require douches, enemas or colostomy irrigations, or requires and receives such service at infrequent intervals for the treatment of a short-term condition.

*4 — Four points are allowed when the recipient requires and receives a douche, enema and/or colostomy irrigation on a regular basis but less than daily.

*5 — Five points when the recipient requires and receives a douche, enema and/or colostomy irrigation *at least daily.*

When enemas are required and given on a regular basis, the patient is not considered, under item 6, to have bowel incontinence.

8. *Diet*

0 — No point is allowed when the diet ordered by the physician is the menu used for the majority of the patients in the facility, with or without minor modifications, such as removal of salt or sugar on trays, substitution of salads or desserts, etc. This includes pureed and baby food, or a mechanical (ground) diet.

*3 — Three points are allowed when the diet ordered by the attending physician is a specific diet which must be prepared separately from the daily menu. This includes salt free, weighed or calculated caloric diets, and diets and tube feedings which require the purchase of special foods.

9. *Medications (Oral, Drops, Ointments, Suppositories)*

If a need for sheltered care is being considered the caseworker will determine whether the recipient is capable of handling his own medication, based on the physician's order, caseworker's knowledge of the recipient, and his past behavior pattern. The attending physician's order regarding the recipient's ability to self-administer medications will be the determining factor in deciding whether a recipient can handle his own medications. In instances where a recipient is taking more than two prescribed medications and is residing in a sheltered care facility, or is being considered for referral to a sheltered care facility, and the physician's order for self-administration does not list all medications being taken, a listing of all medications prescribed for that individiual is to be forwarded to the Regional Medical Assistance Consultant. A brief statement of the recipient's condition, including diagnosis, and the caseworker's recommendation regarding the recipient's capability of handling his own medication is to accompany the list of medications. The Regional Medical Assistance Consultant will review the information and advise the county department in those cases where additional contact with the physician is recommended.

Prescribed PRN and variable dosage medications, controlled substances, and anticoagulants cannot be self-administered in a sheltered care facility.

0 — No point is allowed when medication is not prescribed, or the recipient's condition is such that the physician gives written permission for the resident to handle the medication himself. This includes supervised self-administration in sheltered care facilities.

*1 — One point is allowed for the recipient who requires and receives prescribed medication (oral, drops, ointments, suppositories) administered by staff on a less than daily basis.

*3 — Three points are allowed for the recipient who requires and receives prescribed medication (oral, drops, ointments, suppositories) administered by staff on a *regular daily basis.*

10.   *Injections (Hypodermic and Intramuscular)*

0 — No point is allowed when hypodermics or intramuscular injections have not been prescribed by the physician or when a recipient is permitted to self-administer a drug by hypodermic on the written order of the physician.

*2 — Two points are allowed when hypodermics and/or intramuscular injections are administered on a less than daily basis by a licensed nurse.

*4 — Four points are allowed when the recipient requires and receives a *daily* injection of medication by a licensed nurse *throughout the evaluation period.*

11.   *Intravenous and Subcutaneous Fluids*

0 — No point is allowed when the recipient does not require intravenous or subcutaneous fluids.

*2 — Two points are allowed when the recipient requires and receives intravenous and/or subcutaneous medication or fluids administered by the physician. (This allowance compensates the facility for supplies used.)

\# 8 — Eight points are allowed when intravenous or sub-cutaneous fluids are administered by a registered professional nurse upon the physician's order.

12. *Suctioning*

0 — No point is allowed when the recipient does not require suctioning.

*3 — Three points are allowed when a recipient has a condition, such as a tracheotomy, to which he has become adjusted to such a degree that he is able to care for it himself with minimum assistance by nursing staff for cleansing purposes.

*5 — Five points are allowed when the recipient requires suctioning less than daily.

\# 8 — Eight points are allowed when the recipient requires suctioning *daily throughout the evaluation period.*

13. *Oxygen (Includes Positive Pressure)*

0 — No point is allowed when the recipient has no need for oxygen services.

*4 — Four points are allowed when the recipient requires oxygen on an emergency basis or intermittently during the month. Also included is the recipient who is able to administer his own oxygen and/or positive pressure treatments with supervision and minimum assistance.

\# 8 — Eight points are allowed when there is a current written order, and the recipient receives oxygen and/or positive pressure treatments on a daily basis, administered by nursing staff.

14. *Dressings and Appliances*

0 — No point is allowed when the recipient requires no dressings or requires only an occasional small temporary dressing for minor cuts or abrasions.

*4 — Four points are allowed when the recipient requires daily application of Ace bandages, additional care because of a cast and/or assistance with the application of appliances such as protheses, braces and supports.

*6 — Six points are allowed when the recipient requires dressings to a moderate sized area and/or moist dressings or soaks, on a *continuing* basis. Such services may be required for, but are not limited to: decubiti; recurrent leg ulcers; and daily colostomy dressings.

#8 — Eight points are allowed when there is a physician's written order for comprehensive dressings required on a regular daily basis, performed by an RN or graduate LPN.

15. *Intermediate Care*

* — If services listed above do not indicate a need for either skilled or intermediate care, but the recipient needs services which must be provided or supervised by licensed nursing personnel, then intermediate care is required. When the need for such services is identified by the caseworker or is pointed out by either the attending physician or facility staff and the caseworker verifies the need, a notation of the service which requires the licensed nursing personnel is to be made on the evaluation form and intermediate care is to be authorized. If the caseworker questions the need for licensed nursing personnel, the caseworker will refer the case to the Regional Medical Assistance Consultant for a determination of the level of care required. If intermediate care is approved a notation of the service which requires the licensed nursing personnel is to be made on the authorization form.

16. *Skilled Care*

— If services listed above do not indicate a need for skilled care but the recipient needs 24 hour licensed nursing care or supervision to meet specific needs indicated in his plan for care or an RN is required to assess the patient's needs and prepare the plan for care or a plan for the administration and/or control of medications such as narcotics or dicumerol, skilled

care is required. When the need for such a service is identified by the caseworker or pointed out by the attending physician or facility staff, and the caseworker verifies the need, a notation of the service requiring skilled care is to be made on the evaluation form and skilled care is to be authorized. If the caseworker questions the need for skilled care, the caseworker will refer the case to the Regional Medical Assistance Consultant for a determination of the level of care required. If skilled care is approved a notation of the service requiring skilled care is to be made on the evaluation form.

17. Assistance with bathing: YES ____ NO ____

18. Assistance with dressing: YES ____ NO ____

19. Assistance with grooming: YES ____ NO ____

EVALUATION OF NEED FOR CARE

Name _____*Mrs. W. T.*_____ Case No. _____

A   B   C   D

| 8 | | | |

1. Eating
   0 - Independent
   1 - Requires regular minimum assistance.
   2 - Requires part time assistance by staff.
   4 - Requires constant attendance by staff to hand feed and to insure adequate intake
   #8 - Tube feeding or gastrostomy feeding.

| 2 | | | |

2. Mobility
   0 - Requires no assistance or is independent with assistive devices
   2 - Mobile with assistance.
   *3 - Completely dependent upon staff or condition is such that more than one staff member is required to give assistance.

| 3 | | | |

3. Behavior and Mental Condition
   0 - Adequate mental and social functioning within the facility.
   3 - Requires occasional supervision due to behavioral and mental condition.
   *8 - Requires frequent or constant direction and guidance due to servere behavioral or mental condition.

| 12 | | | |

4. Physical Rehabilitation Needs
   0 - No potential for rehabilitation
   *4 - Needs and is receiving rehabilitation services to maintain current level of function.
   *8 - Needs and is receiving intensive rehabilitation services to improve functioning directly related to selected acute illnesses or injuries within the period of 3 to 6 months following discharge (*allow 8 points only if facility has an approved rehabilitation nursing program*)
   *12 - Needs and is receiving intensive rehabilitation services to improve functioning directly related to selected acute illnesses or injuries during the three month period following discharge. (*allow 12 points only if facility has an approved rehabilitation nursing program*)

5. Catheterization *(including irrigations)*
   0 - Never
   *4 - Occasional, for specimen and for short time treatment.
   *8 - Continuous retention catheter will full care.

6. Incontinence *(bladder and bowel)*
   0 - None
   1 - May have occasional accidents
   2 - Partial bowel or bladder incontinence
   8 - Maintenance following a training program
   *6 - Total bowel and/or bladder incontinence
   *8 - Bowel and bladder training program *(six month limitation)*

7. Douches, Enemas or Colostomy Irrigations
   0 - None or occasional
   *4 - Less than daily
   *5 - Daily

8. Diet
   0 - Regular, soft, bland or low salt
   3 - Other special diets as ordered by physician

9. Medications *(oral, ointments, drops and suppositories)*
   0 - Never
   1 - Less than daily
   3 - Daily

111 184b (N-2-74)

A   B   C   D

10. Injections *(hypodermic and tramuscular)*
    0 - Never
    *2 - Irregular *(points may be allowed in sheltered care home)*
    *4 - Daily *(points may be allowed in sheltered care homes)*

11. Intravenous and Subcutaneous Fluids
    0 - Never
    2 - Given by Physician
    #8 - Given by R.N. on physician's orders

12. Suctioning
    0 - Never
    *3 - Self-care or with minimum assistance
    *5 - Less than daily
    #8 - Daily

13. Oxygen *(includes positive pressure)*
    0 - Never
    *4 - Less than daily or with minimum assistance
    #8 - Daily

14. Dressings and Appliances
    0 - None or occasional small dressing for minor cuts or abrasions.
    *4 - Regular application of appliances and/or Ace bandages, or care required because of a cast.
    *6 - Dressings to moderate size areas.
    #8 - Comprehensive dressings needed regularly.

#*15. The recipient requires nursing care 24 hours a day for selected acute illness or injuries. *(This care may be provided in an ICF I if the facility is staffed and equipped to provide the necessary care)*, or skilled nursing care was recommended as a result of a medical review conducted by IDPH.

#* Except where otherwise specified, points are not allowed in sheltered care homes for these procedures.

	Evaluation (A) Date *12/4/1*	Evaluation (B) Date _____	Evaluation (C) Date _____	Evaluation (D) Date _____
Needs Assistance With: *(Circle One)* Bathing	YES NO	YES NO	YES NO	YES NO
(Circle One) Dressing	YES NO	YES NO	YES NO	YES NO
(Circle One) Grooming	YES NO	YES NO	YES NO	YES NO
Total Point Count	44			
•Level of Care Needed	Skilled			
MONTHLY RATE				
DAILY RATE				
EFFECTIVE DATE				

FACILITY NAME:
    ADDRESS:
    I. D. #

APPROVALS:
    ( ) Shelter Factor
    ( ) Rehabilitation Nursing
    ( ) Activity Program
    ( ) Social Rehabilitation

Appendix D

Implementation Plan for the Quality Assurance Program: As Developed for First Healthcare Corporation

Elapsed Months

0 1 2 3 4 5 6 7 8 9 10 11 12

Task 1.0 - Develop the master plan for quality assurance programs

1.01 - Overview paper for introduction of the concepts subsequently to be developed in detail in 1.1 and 1.2

1.1 - Part A - Concurrent Review Program

  1.11 - Develop "Overview" of this program

  1.12 - Develop detailed, step by step procedure description

    1.121 - Computer Application

1.2 - Part B - Retrospective Review

  1.21 - Develop overview of this program

  1.22 - Develop detailed, step-by-step-procedure description

  1.23 - Develop Corporation-wide program

    1.231 - Computer Application

  1.24 - Educational feedback system (see task 7.0)

Task 2.0 - Develop formal statement of the Utilization Review Plan:

  2.1 - As included in 1.12

  2.2 - As required by Medicare

  2.3 - As required by Medicaid

  2.4 - As results in "due care status"

  2.5 - As it relates to PSRO

  2.6 - As it relates to cost reimbursement model

Elapsed
Months
0 1 2 3 4 5 6 7 8 9 10 11 12

Task 3.0 - Implementation strategy
   3.1 - Develop Corporate Patient Care
      Committee
      3.11 - Review of QAP
      3.12 - Revision of QAP
   3.2 - Testing program
      3.21 - Select test sites
      3.22 - Implement programs in test
          sites
      3.23 - Evaluate programs
      3.24 - Revision of QAP
   3.3 - Regional Orientation Program
      designed

      3.31 - Regional implementation
         3.311 - Regional conference (See
            Task 4.2)
   3.4 - Institutional Orientation Pro-
      grams (on regional basis)
      3.41 - Evaluate "readiness" to start
         Task 5.0

Task 4.0 - Implement concept of goal-
oriented nursing care
   4.1 - Develop Educational/Imple-
      mental package for institutional
      use
      4.11 - Test packages (See Tasks 3.22,
         3.23)
      4.12 - Revise packages (See Task
         3.24)
   4.2 - Regional Orientation Conference
      (coordinate with Task 3.311)

Task 5.0 - Implement Part A, QAP (Concurrent Review)
   5.1 - Implement Utilization Review
      Plan (See Task 2.0)

Task 6.0 - Implement Part B, QAP
(Retrospective Review) (See Task 1.2)

Task 7.0 - Implement Corporate - Regional
- Instutional In-service educational network
   7.1 - Design network
   7.2 - Develop educational methodolo-
      gies

Elapsed
Months

	0	1	2	3	4	5	6	7	8	9	10	11	12

7.3 - Develop educational resources

7.31 - Program development

7.32 - Audio-visual materials

7.4 - Develop evaluation mechanism

Task 8.0 - Implement Rehabilitative/ Restorative Nursing Care Education Program (Using system implemented in Task 7.0)

8.1 - Train regional nurse coordinators (courses, etc.)

8.2 - Develop FHC educational package

8.3 - Implement package

8.4 - Implement reality orientation package

Task 9.0 - Extend QAP to management areas, pharmacy, dietary, housekeeping, plant maintenance, engineering

Index

211

About the Author

Thomas H. Ainsworth, Jr., M.D. is medical director and director of Hospital Education Programs of Illinois Masonic Medical Center. He is Professor of Clinical Surgery, University of Illinois, Abraham Lincoln School of Medicine. He is a board-certified general surgeon, and as a Fellow of the American College of Surgeons serves as a member of their Commission on Cancer. He practiced general surgery for 20 years in suburban Philadelphia, where he served as Chief of General Surgery at the Bryn Mawr Hospital. In 1952 he established one of the first intensive care units in the country and later developed the patient care committee and home care program at Bryn Mawr. While a practicing surgeon, he served as the Chairman of the Council on Extended Care for the Hospital Association of Pennsylvania for three years and served on many committees, advisory panels, and the Council on Professional Services of the American Hospital Association.

His residency training at N.Y.U.-Bellevue Medical Center has provided a background in the problems of large municipal hospitals. While practicing in Philadelphia, he also taught at Temple University School of Medicine, where he was clinical associate professor of surgery and clinical associate professor of anatomy. Serving as the AHA's representative to the Administrative Board of the Council of Teaching Hospitals of the Association of American Medical Colleges, he has been intimately aware of the problems of the academic medical center and its teaching hospitals.

In September of 1970, at the age of 50, Doctor Ainsworth left the active practice of surgery to join the American Hospital Association as associate director. In this position he organized the Committee on Physicians and served as the first chairman of this board of trustees committee. Doctor Ainsworth established *The Hospital Medical Staff* journal and served as its first editor. He represented the AHA in the formation of the Coordinating Council on Medical Education and the Liaison Committee on Graduate Medical Education and served as staff representative of the AHA to these two councils, as well as maintaining constant liaison with all national medical organizations, including the American Medical Association, American Board of Medical Specialties, American Academy of Family Practice, American College of Physicians, American College of Surgeons, and the Joint Commission on Accreditation of Hospitals. He also served as a consultant on the Steering Committee for the Experimental Medical Care Review Organization (EMCRO) projects for the National Center for Health Services Research and Development for a two-year period. He has maintained active liaison with governmental agencies within the Department of Health, Education, and Welfare.

Doctor Ainsworth is the editor and principal author of the *Quality Assurance Program for Medical Care in the Hospital.* He also served on the AMA's Task Force on Rules and Regulations for Professional Standards Review Organizations (PSRO). He is a board member of the Cook County (Chicago) PSRO and serves on their committee on delegated review. He is a member of the Council on Patient Care, Illinois Hospital Association and a board member of the Illinois Cooperative Health Data System.